# THESE BODIES

*The Worship God Wants*

**Apostle Terri Andres**

HARVESTER PUBLISHING
ATLANTA, GA

Copyright © 2023 by Terri Andres

All rights reserved. No part of this publication may be reproduced, distributed, or transmitted in any form or by any means, including photocopying, recording, or other electronic or mechanical methods, without the prior written permission of the publisher, except in the case of brief quotations embodied in critical reviews and certain other noncommercial uses permitted by copyright law. For permission requests, write to the publisher, addressed "Attention: Permissions Coordinator," at the address below.

**Terri Andres/Harvester Publishing**
4780 Ashford Dunwoody Road
Atlanta, GA 30338
www.harvester-publishing.com

Unless otherwise indicated, all scripture quotations are from the Holy Bible, New King James Version®, NKJV® Copyright © 1982 Thomas Nelson. Used with permission. All rights reserved.

Book Cover Design by Tanja Prokop
Book Layout © 2017 BookDesignTemplates.com

THESE BODIES™/ Terri Andres -- 1st ed. *Unabridged*
ISBN 978-1-7351862-2-1

*Dedicated to all spiritual sons and daughters of YHWH living in this present world.*

*Therefore, when Christ came into the world, he said:
"Sacrifice and offering you did not desire, but a body
you prepared for me."*

—HEBREWS 10:5 (NIV)

# CONTENTS

FOREWORD ................................................................. i
PREFACE ..................................................................... ii
INTRODUCTION ........................................................ 1
GOD WANTS YOUR BODY ...................................... 7
THESE BODIES 101 .................................................. 13
THESE BODIES REVELATIONS ............................. 27
THESE BODIES TEACHINGS ................................. 41
THESE BODIES IN SCRIPTURE ............................. 67
THESE BODIES CONDITION ................................. 79
THESE BODIES REMEDY ....................................... 91
THESE BODIES AND OUR WORSHIP ................ 109
THESE BODIES INVITATION .............................. 133
THESE BODIES FINAL THOUGHTS ................... 147
AUTHOR NOTE ..................................................... 175
CLIFF NOTES ......................................................... 177
PERSONAL NOTES ............................................... 185
INDEX ..................................................................... 203

# FOREWORD

Dear reader. While authors do not usually write the forewords to their own books, in my book (literally and figuratively), spiritual importance overrules formality as I feel it to be of the utmost importance to provide you with a sense of the atmosphere in which this prophetic message began to unfold.

I was driving home from work less than .4 miles away from my driveway gate when, suddenly, Holy Spirit overshadowed me and started speaking to me about THESE BODIES. His voice was so clear and strong I had no other choice but to detour off the main road to find the nearest parking space so I could write down what He was saying.

After driving down a familiar street and several turns later, I found myself parked in the back of a PF Chang's restaurant frantically writing. I could not write fast enough. I wrote and wrote, only looking up and around occasionally at the security officer that was checking me out the whole time.

**APOSTLE TERRI ANDRES**

Three hours later – now dark with streetlights on – I started my car ignition to finally head home. This marked the beginning of subsequent supernatural writing sessions, too many to count, strong over the next several years.

# PREFACE

This THESE BODIES message for the Bride and Body of Christ was first spoken to me by Holy Spirit in March of 2018 and consistently throughout the years that follow up until the release of this 1st edition in November 2023. Five years later. Five the number of grace.

While the text has undergone light editing for the purposes of acceptable reading comprehension and book formatting, the integrity of exactly what Holy Spirit spoke to me has been preserved – hence releasing the message unabridged.

Lastly, understand this message is prophetic not in the sense of foretelling some thing or some event, but rather prophetic in the sense of telling forth what has already been revealed to us in the Word of God but tragically not widely preached and therefore practiced.

Apostle Terri Andres

# INTRODUCTION

When a couple wants to have a baby, the fact of the matter is what they really want is to have a body. When a baby is born, the fact of the matter is a body is born. When we refer to human beings, the fact of the matter is we are really referring to human bodies. When we talk about mankind, we are really talking about bodies of men, women, and children. When someone dies, the fact of the matter is their body dies.

Have you ever wondered what qualifies you (us) to exist and live in this world?

The answer is your body. My body. Our bodies. THESE BODIES.

These bodies of ours qualify and enable us to exist and live in the physical world. It is not possible for natural, biological human beings to be alive in this physical world without a physical body.

As elementary as it is, before the LORD began revealing this message, I had not given it any real earnest thought.

## APOSTLE TERRI ANDRES

What I have since come to realize, and I pray you will too, is that having a keen awareness and thorough understanding of the spiritual and physical truths about THESE BODIES, and related aspects, is of the utmost importance in order for us to use THESE BODIES to exist and rule in this current age as our Creator intends. As well as to understand and thus prepare for the ultimate purpose of THESE BODIES which lies ahead of us in the new order to come. Eternity.

This message is a means to this end. A prophetic revelation to raise your consciousness and, moreover, unveil truth about THESE BODIES of ours.

The deep and powerful truths shared here are purposed to awaken, liberate, heal, deliver, redeem, and endue resurrection power into your being and body that is one in the same.

The Bride and Body of Christ today is, by and large, powerless over sin. I believe the number one reason for this is lack of knowledge and lack of revelation of the spiritual truths and testimony (Word) of God in the person of Jesus Christ.

In case you haven't heard, the Bible is a spiritual book, full of spiritual truths of a spiritual Godhead that rules and reigns over a spiritual Kingdom of spiritual sons and daughters who make up the Bride and Body of Christ — the Church. The *ekklesia*, those who are the called-out ones.

Tragically, "the Church" of God today consist of many Christian leader influencers with megachurches and mass social media followings who have and continue to fail in rightly dividing the scriptures, ultimately because of their own misaligned hearts with the heart and plans of our heavenly Father and His Kingdom. Their self-centered bible teachings are largely oriented to align with achieving the organization's marketing, financial and operating objectives in order to keep their churches full and growing instead of spiritual transformation messages and the making and multiplying of disciples and the practical equipping that should accompany these messages.

Second to this lack of knowledge within the Bride and Body of Christ is dividedness of heart between loving God and loving the world. Now I firmly believe most of our brothers and sisters do love God and want to obey Him and do good works. Absolutely. The problem is they do not love God, want to obey Him and do good works *over and above* self and the things of the world. Mammon. Because of this, the latter wins out because we all know well it is impossible to serve both God and mammon.

More tragically, but not surprisingly because the Word warns us this will be the case, by and large, the leadership focus of this present generation of Christian believers is on building Christian businesses with obscene income and assets first before building the Bride and Body of Christ which is a spiritual household of spiritual sons and daughters without spot or blemish. Let's be crystal clear here. A spiritual house without spot or blemish is the Bride Christ is coming back for. Not anything else.

And along the lines of the eminent Second Coming of Christ, or *Parousia*, for His Church and our present error, misalignment, and shortcomings (because of His grace, goodness, and mercy), the will, counsel and Word of the LORD for His Church and Kingdom will prevail. This we can be sure of, stand on and look forward to with great anticipation and enthusiasm. Our gracious LORD always provides a ram in the bush, raises up a Saul, a David, a Daniel, a Deborah, a John, a Mary, an apostle Paul.

And today, for such a time as this, when the end is nearer than it has ever been and when we are living in perilous times, He raises up a you and a me to speak through to first His Church and second to this dark and dying world to bring them into the fold. Hallelujah amen.

## WHAT THIS MESSAGE WILL RENDER

This message has the power to set you free from the bondage of sin and death in order to exist and operate in the Spirit of life in Christ. What this means is existing and experiencing in this life everything good and godly your heart and soul long for. Being and living free from inner struggles you have been bound by all your life. Freedom from fears, offenses, unforgiveness, anger, hatred, guilt, shame and condemnation. Freedom from bad habits and addictions. Freedom from pride, selfishness, and self-centeredness. Freedom from insecurities, rejection, doubt, and confusion. Freedom from fear of going without and not having your basic needs met. Freedom from worry and broken relationships with people you love but can't fix. Freedom from attachment to anything in this world. Freedom from the love of money and material possessions. Freedom from forever reaching and striving for that something you can't quite put your finger on to articulate, but you know in your spirit you need it in order to be whole and complete in this life. Freedom from it all — the bondage of sin and death.

This message will immediately or in time open your eyes and/or deepen your understanding of the spiritual depthness and relevance present in the Word of God. This message will expose the error of the majority of Christian messages widely preached and taught today that are self-centered and worldly with zero resemblance to the teachings of our LORD Jesus Christ. Correct error. Convict evil and dark deeds by shedding the Light of Truth on them. Lead you to repentance. Provide practical application and steps for being and living the life you are meant to live in your body – to become a spiritual being, which is to become like God.

*Whole, free, powerful, and victorious in every aspect of your being, body, and behavior.*

# GOD WANTS YOUR BODY

How many times have you heard a message about how God wants your heart? That God wants your head and your heart. That God wants all of you – spirit, soul and body. That God wants every part of your soul – mind, will and emotions?

If your experience has been like mine, you have heard these types of messages too many times to count. Also, on the other hand, if your experience has been like mine, you have never heard a message where "God wants your body" is emphasized or expounded upon as much as the others. Instead, it was merely glossed over.

In over 26 years of consistently walking with the LORD and hearing hundreds of sermons on Sundays as well as throughout the week, I had not and still have not to this very day.

Yet the Word of God reveals this truth and makes it very clear that our bodies are the *acceptable* (keyword) worship God wants from us.

Which of course brings us to Romans 12:1-2, a familiar passage of scripture that you can probably quote because you have heard many sermons on it.

Before receiving deeper revelation, I understood Romans 12:1-2 mainly in the context of presenting my body as a living sacrifice. The interpretation of my mind as to what this looked like practically was: 1) consecrating my body unto Him; 2) consistently denying my flesh in some form to sacrifice and put it to death ("a living sacrifice"); and 3) thinking and behaving different from the world – living a holy, obedient life.

Before going further, I want to note these thoughts of being a living sacrifice are good for what they are and would absolutely honor God while also rendering benefits to you/your body and your faith walk. However, we must not ever shrink from earnestly seeking to rightly divide Scripture through deep study and meditation in order to obtain the truths, mysteries of old that are now revealed, knowledge and wisdom of God.

Moving on, it is interesting that for many years (twenty-plus) of walking consistently with the LORD, staying in the Word and living a sacrificial and devoted life of service to Him, the revelation of the *acceptable* worship He wants never hit me. Again, it was always the three things I named. However, in retrospect, my spirit always sensed there was more.

I recall all the cross-reference and commentary studies, all the meditating and mulling over seeking the true meaning of what this passage was really saying. And while I'd arrived at some inkling about "the body part," it was overshadowed by the traditional picture of worship which is made up of singing praises, soaking in worship experiences, private devotion, and commitment to living set apart and sacrificially serving God.

*Until* that special day in March 2018 when He decided to start revealing this message.

I don't know about you, but the God I know and serve is always on time with His plans – past, present, and future. He revealed His Truth to me when He wanted to and He chose me to share it with you now.

## ACCEPTABLE WORSHIP

What is acceptable worship in THESE BODIES and what does it look like? In a few sentences, acceptable worship is the offering of spiritual sacrifices to God while living in your physical body. Sacrifices only your inner spiritual man can offer. Like becoming spiritual, which is being like Him and acting like Him. Keyword, like. Likeness. We are made in His image and likeness.

Acceptable worship is aligning your heart (desires) and mind with His heart and mind – which is essentially John's baptism of repentance. Having a heart and mind turned away from the spirit of this world and turned to the Kingdom of God. The offering up of spiritual sacrifices such as obedience and the wielding over of your entire being so the Spirit of Christ can live, move and have His being in you versus sacrifices from your outer man like going to church, clapping your hands and shouting *hallelujah amen*. Or "good works" sacrifices from your outer man like serving in this ministry or that ministry. Again, while outer man sacrifices are often good and godly, God is first and foremost after something else for *acceptable* worship to Him. That something else being that which is spiritual.

Spiritual sacrifices are the only sacrifices we can offer God because God is a Spirit and they that worship Him must worship Him in spirit and in truth. See John 4:24.

Now it is important to note. This does not mean our bodies do not play a role in the offering of spiritual sacrifices to God. On the contrary, they absolutely do. Not only does God want our bodies – as the title of this chapter indicates – He *needs* our bodies.

> *God needs our bodies to perform His works of righteousness through us in the earth and His will is to use our bodies to perform His works of righteousness when we are a) like Him and b) joined to Him.*

*Like Him* as in spiritual like Him (yes, I am being a bit repetitive but stay with me). Born of Him. Spiritually alive. Having a spiritual nature like His that rule over the carnal sin nature. *Joined to Him* by the presence and power of Holy Spirit living in us. It is Holy Spirit and only Holy Spirit that enables and empowers us to be righteous, behave righteous, and live righteously by God's righteous standards.

Also, as a worthy mention and clarity, Holy Spirit the third Person of the Godhead, should not be confused with the breath (spirit) of God that gives life to our physical bodies and all flesh.

The Person of Holy Spirit gives us the Righteousness of God and continually works to separate us from sin and fills us with *dunamis* (Strongs NT 1411 δύναμις). Miraculous power, might and strength. Power through God's ability. This divine power enables us to exercise the rule and authority of Christ over our sin nature (flesh), demons and demonic activity, and to resist temptation. Hear me sons and daughters of the Most High God when I say this:

> *We need dunamis power in every area of our self and life outside of self to grow in sanctification by which we are prepared for glorification.*

In conclusion, this brief introduction of acceptable worship is but a scratch on the surface. Given this entire book is about this one subject, know it will be thoroughly unpacked, or better stated, revealed, from this point forward.

# 2

# THESE BODIES 101

I named this chapter as such because what I am going to share here is exactly what God revealed to me first when He overshadowed me on my way home from work that day in March of 2018. If you have not done so already, flip back and read the foreword of the book for the short backstory about this.

While I do not know why God started revealing this message with these points first, I trust Him and know it was not only for good reason but for purposeful reason because His nature includes strategy and order.

Therefore, open your heart and mind to receive this as vital heavenly POV (point-of-view) about THESE BODIES without judgment or opinion. Just receive the message for what it is. Also, to be clear, when I say *heavenly*, as in from our heavenly Father which makes this imperative to digest. Resist any tendency to read fast to get to what's next. As an avid reader, I know finishing a book cover-to-cover as fast as possible is often an underlying goal so we can experience that major shot of dopamine from the achievement of doing so.

Instead, feed slowly after first asking Holy Spirit to touch you and open the spirit of your mind to clearly receive what He speaks and imparts to you. If you are a speed-reader, I encourage you to read this repeatedly.

## HEAVENLY POV ABOUT THESE BODIES

POV is an acronym for Point-of-View. The points that follow are the original points God gave me – and *how* He gave them to me – when He first started downloading this message to me in the car driving home that evening.

- What we do in these bodies is *everything*.

- Our bodies enable us and qualify us to exist in this physical world.

- Our bodies have specific purposes:
    o To be a dwelling place for God's Spirit
    o To be (reflect) the glory of God
    o To worship, praise and thank God
    o To procreate
    o To create, work and rule over all other creation
    o To receive love and give love

- To submit to the superior inner man that is joined to God (for those in Christ through His Spirit)
- To give of yourself – time, talents and treasure

- Because of sin, our bodies are defective and non-fixable:
    - Corrupt
    - Totally depraved
    - Prone to sickness and disease
    - Mortal (subject to physical death)

- Our bodies are in the process of dying from birth because of the transmission and presence of sin.
    - As we age (the older we get), sin abounds and the wages of sin is physical death of our bodies

- Our physical bodies are separated from and keep us separate from our creator God, who is a Spirit. Our spirit (which is what was made in the image and likeness of God) is what joins us to the Godhead – Father, Son, Holy Spirit.

- Death of our physical bodies is a doorway to freedom. Final freedom and liberation of our corrupted bodies.

- Our physical bodies are not intended for:
    - Sexual immorality/sexual pleasure outside of marriage between a man and woman
    - Gratification from food
    - Gratification from drugs/alcohol

15

- - Gratification from artificial stimulants
  - Gratification from digital images and videos that arouse and excite physical senses and certain body parts
- Our physical bodies are enslaved to sin and only able to be free from this enslavement by becoming a living sacrifice by the power of Holy Spirit's work in us, empowering us to constantly put to death our sinful nature. Which lends itself to us constantly decreasing so He can fully operate in us unencumbered by our self and selfish will.
- Our physical bodies are the lowest part of our being (yet we act as if they are the highest. We put forth our highest and best effort and striving into how they look).
  - We are triune beings: spirit, soul and body
  - Our bodies are inferior to our spirit and soul (the unseen, superior aspects of our being)
  - Therefore, since the body is the most inferior part of us, our spirit/soul should control it and not the other way around where our corrupted, depraved physical body controls/rules spirit and soul
- Our physical bodies are fragile and weak.
  - Example: too high of a temperature will burn our bodies; too low of a temperature will

THESE BODIES

freeze our bodies; too hard of a blow to our head or certain part of the body can put us to death or damage us permanently

- Our physical bodies are docile.
  - Readily trained or taught
  - Submissive
    - Because it is not intelligent in and of itself; on its own
    - It submits to the training it receives; the input; the conditioning

- Our physical bodies are trained by its intake (what it consumes) and this:
  - Determines your overall experience in your body
  - Determines your overall experience in the world (because of the condition of your body)
  - Largely determines your natural longevity ("natural" because accidents happen)
  - Consequences of our intake are one of two things: *good or bad*

- What our physical bodies consume has serious consequences (whether good consequences or bad consequences).
  - Our intake affects our triune being: spirit, soul and body

17

- o Our intake determines our spiritual state/condition while living in this physical world: good or evil; light or darkness

- God became a physical body in the Person of Jesus Christ to defeat physical death so those who believe in Him and thereby receive His victory over physical death, will themselves have victory over the physical death of their body and be raised up to new eternal life with a new spiritual body absent the corruption of his or her current body of sin that *must* die physically.

- When Christ lived in a body, His physical intake was limited. He fed off bread from heaven (see John 6). *Spiritual meat* was His main food, knowing His core identity was that of a spirit and that His physical body was born to die, He did not feed (gorge/overconsume) on the things of this world that are physical/seen. Rather, His consumption was predominantly spiritual and unseen. This, He knew, was profitable.

- When we refer to "our life," what we are really referring to is our life in a physical body.
    - o This is a key fundamental principle to understand as well as catch in the spirit
    - o Without our physical bodies, it is impossible for us to exist in this present world we know

- A body is born, a body dies
 - Our spirits existed/exists/will exist in eternity past, eternity present and eternity future

- The key to victory in these bodies is to become spirit strong.
 - There are very specific things we *must* do
 - Christ settled the matter of our corrupt, defective and depraved flesh that is destined to die by making a public spectacle of death through the death of His sinless body

- When we become nothing and lower and humble ourselves in THESE BODIES we win. When we make ourselves somebody full of pride and puffed-up, we inevitably become bound.
 - Sin has no power over a lowly nobody because how can a dead man sin? He cannot according to Romans 6:7
 - Sin has all power over a puffed-up somebody because of the sin that has the opportunity to abound through pride. Sin lives in us, is acted out through us and is therefore all around us

- What we do in these physical bodies is our *acceptable* (or not) worship to God our creator and maker.
   - Acceptable (keyword) worship to God is not going to a church building on Sunday or a particular day of the week

- Nor is it only clapping, singing, and having a worship-like experience with music, singing, etc.

- Acceptable worship is what we do and don't do in THESE BODIES while we exist in physical form and in this realm of time. Such as:
  - Our devotion to God and His Kingdom or devotion to the kingdom/spirit of the world
  - How we use our time consistently
  - What we look at consistently
  - What we think about, meditate and dwell on consistently
  - What we consume consistently
  - What we act out, what we do and don't do consistently
  - The sacrifices we make such as not over-indulging on food and raw feel pleasures; sacrificing our own comfort before our service to others; sacrificial giving for the glory of God and building His Kingdom; etc.

- To sacrifice is to be and thus behave spiritual. Said another way, when we sacrifice our self/flesh, we are existing as spiritual beings and behaving as spiritual beings. When we sacrifice self and give to

**THESE BODIES**

others, we are existing as spiritual beings like our God, who is a Spirit, who *sacrificed* and *gave* Himself

- We must present our bodies as living sacrifices. Sin lives in us. When we live as dead, decrease, the Holy Spirit of God (all His power, virtue and strength) increases and lives, moves and has His being in us and empowers us to rule over sin and temptation unto holiness, righteousness and good works.

- Our bodies are made to be the dwelling place for the Holy Spirit of God.
    - His Holy dwelling. His Holy temple that takes the place of the former temple structures from the Old Covenant. His Holy abode in our body

    - His abode in THESE BODIES. His abode in THESE BODIES. His abode in THESE BODIES

    - Why? So the Holy Spirit can work and be active everywhere. No longer in one central place in a Jerusalem temple but throughout the earth to the ends of the earth. The bible confirms this with its profound teaching that the body is meant for the LORD and the LORD for the body

APOSTLE TERRI ANDRES

## SOME BASIC TRUTHS FOR CHRISTIANS

In conclusion of this chapter, THESE BODIES 101, I will present basic statements of truth about our faith that, if you are a professing Christian, you should not only know of these truths but have a solid comprehension of these truths in order to, first and foremost, be able to apply them to your walk with the LORD and secondly, as a disciple of Christ, share them with others when an occasion calls for it.

Note this is by no means an exhaustive list of basic truths – far from it. This is what was given to me by Holy Spirit while receiving from Him and subsequently writing the message of THESE BODIES.

### SIN NATURE

The words: body; body of sin; flesh; sin; and self can be thought of as synonymous. All of these words can be used interchangeably because they all make up the sin nature of our physical bodies. So, what we have is Body=Body of Sin=Flesh=Sin=Self=Sin Nature.

### DEATH OF SELF

Dying to self (the body of sin) – no longer pleasing, feeding, gratifying – is the only road to liberty in our bodies that have natures to sin because of total corruptness outside of the indwelling Spirit of Christ.

### ALIVE IN CHRIST

Christ becomes our stead over self. As our spirits are more and more drawn to Christ/Holy Spirit by our submission of our will and obedience to Him/His will/Word/laws/commands/instructions, we increase in Him. He increases in us. His power increases in us. His anointing increases in us. We become joined to Him. Bound to Him like super glue. United. One. At peace with Him.

### CHRIST IN US

Christ's death justifies us. Christ's Spirit sanctifies us. Christ's Second Coming will glorify us – new spiritual bodies absent of sin and corruption. Perfect triune beings (spirit, soul and body) in the image and likeness of our God – Father, Son and Holy Spirit.

### IN THE IMAGE OF CHRIST

What does it really mean to be conformed to the image of Christ? It is increasing from glory to glory. We are literally being made, molded, shaped, conformed to look like Him. To exist and act like Him. According to 1 John 4:17 KJV, as He is, so are we in this world. While in the body, we are continually being made like Him. As He is in eternity, we will be *fully spiritual* like Him.

### FREE IN CHRIST

Christ freed us (and keeps us free by the continual working of His power in us) by becoming our Way of escape from self. When we are without Christ, we are all self. When we are with Christ, He draws us away from self to Himself by His Spirit, Holy Spirit. As our spirit-man is drawn to Christ, we move further and further away from self. We stop feeding self. We stop gratifying self. We stop pleasing self. We stop exalting self. We are free indeed.

## MORE THAN MERELY HUMAN

Carnal, of the flesh, is one facet of the nature of man. That man is a triune being, we must understand the truth and revelation that we – those possessed by the Spirit of God – are more than mere humans. We can be supernatural, citizens of heaven that live from and by the power of our unseen selves. That is, from our spirits. This will only happen when we are filled with the Holy Spirit of God and thereby become spirit strong.

## SPIRIT STRONG

As spiritual sons and daughters (heirs) of God in Christ Jesus, from a natural perspective, as oxymoronic as it may sound, our overarching goal while living in THESE BODIES is to be Spirit Strong™.

For your spirit-man to be stronger than your natural-man and thereby enabling you to be and behave spiritually. Living from your spirit by the power of Holy Spirit. Remember, it is our inner spirit-man that becomes joined to the Spirit of God – which is why the bible teaches and instructs us to move from babes in

Christ to mature adults in Him. This maturation is the process of spiritual transformation. First, born of water (natural man) and, second, born again of God (enlivened spirit man).

The *what, when, where, why,* and *how* to become Spirit Strong™ is an in-depth teaching separate from this message, but suffice it to say here, the only true and acceptable worship to God is what we do in THESE BODIES as spiritual beings. Spiritual sons and daughters behaving spiritually. The Spirit of Christ increasing more and more to strengthen our spirit and self decreasing more and more to weaken our flesh. Which results in slaves to righteousness, no longer slaves to self, sin and unrighteousness.

## DEEP AND VITAL REVELATION

Lastly, from this point forward as you continue reading this prophetic message of THESE BODIES, as well as in your walk and transformation into a spiritual son or daughter (heir) of God in Christ, I encourage you to keep the following deep and vital revelation relative to this message top of mind:

> *The fact that a physical body (Christ's body) had to be born human/a man and die for the redemption of our bodies; our victory; our freedom from the slavery and bondage of sin, evil and demonic oppression.*

**APOSTLE TERRI ANDRES**

See Hebrews 10:5-10, New International Version. Christ Jesus — God incarnate in human flesh — came and dwelt and walked among us. How? *In a physical body.* He put on human flesh. His flesh, however, was the only human flesh that was not corrupted because of sin, which is how we ourselves are redeemed and His Spirit able to abide in us in this fallen world.

Since He, His Body, was crucified, buried, resurrected, and ascended into heaven (His glorified body ascended into heaven) and is no longer in the earth, He gave/gives us His Spirit (capital S for Holy Spirit) by becoming one with our spirits (small s) so He can finish the work He started. Perfecting His children to be like Him and co-labor with Him in the work of the redemption of humanity for the future new heaven and new earth. When paradise lost will be restored. Where old things will pass away and all things will be made new.

# 3

# THESE BODIES REVELATIONS

Shortly after Holy Spirit began revealing the big view of this message to me, He started filling in the details with revelation after revelation. And, of course, I started recording them by hand writing them in the blue spiral notebook I had dedicated for this — a notebook I considered to be consecrated, sacred, holy and, thus, heavily guarded.

Following is all of them the way they were given to me, in order, over the course of a few months back in March of 2018. There are some that was given years later so for these I have included the month and year I received it. These dates may prove insightful for someone reading this in terms of related revelations Holy Spirit may have revealed to you around that time.

### TRIUNITY REDEMPTION AND FREEDOM

Triune God: Father, Son, and Holy Spirit. Triune Man: Spirit, Soul, and Body. Our spirit aligns with the

Father. Our souls align with Christ. Our Bodies align with Holy Spirit. Through redemption (faith and belief) in Christ:

1. We are made alive spiritually after spiritual death from The Fall.
2. Our souls rescued from eternal damnation.
3. We are empowered to rule over sin
4. We are freed from slavery and bondage to sin in these corrupt, mortal bodies.

The Holy Spirit has been given to us as a deposit/seal for the Day of Judgment ("that Day") where when we receive our resurrected bodies according to the promise that the resurrected Christ is the firstborn of many brethren. We will have new spiritual bodies.

The Holy Spirit has not only been given to us for future resurrection unto eternal life but, another profound truth is, in time in THESE BODIES we are joined to Holy Spirit. Joined to Him. One with Him. Which is why it is written: *in Him I live, move, and have my being.*

## FAST TRUTHS ABOUT THESE BODIES

- Our bodies enable us to exist in this physical life. When they die, our spirits live on. The body cannot live without the spirit. It is the Spirit that gives life.

- Our bodies are meant for us to be fruitful and multiply, and:
    - To dominate and subdue the earth
    - To create, like God does
    - To give, like God does
    - To sacrifice, like God does
    - To increase in wisdom, knowledge of Truth, patience and all the fruits of the Spirit, like God
- Our bodies were never and are not now meant to be fed constantly; to constantly consume food, drugs, alcohol, casual sex, entertainment, etc.
- Our bodies were never and are not now made for the above abuse we do to them.
- Our appetite/cravings cause these abusive behaviors in THESE BODIES.

The word appetite traces back to *soul*. So, our souls are the real culprit and cause of abuse – which, in short, is why Christ came to rescue our souls. To save our souls, by the quickening (making alive) of our spirits that were made in His image and likeness, but died and thus separated from God our Maker as a result of the Fall of Man. He quickens us (our spirit) so we can be joined to His Spirit that gives us power over the fallen and therefore corrupt parts of ourselves (heart/mind, soul and body). Read this repeatedly until it sinks in.

The quickening of our spirits is the doctrine of regeneration, or being born again, aka born of God, aka born of the Spirit.

## THE INFERIORITY AND CRAVINGS OF THESE BODIES

The body, THESE BODIES of ours, is the most inferior part of our being. They are the lowest, basest part of it. The closest to beasts. And, as we know, it is the human mind that make us like God our Maker. The mind is a part of the soul of man which is comprised of mind, will, emotions, imagination, and intellect.

When we end up feeding and feeding and endlessly feeding these sick, low, base, animalistic and corrupt bodies, they end up ruling our being with its lusts and cravings and ungodly, insatiable appetites for everything sinful, pleasurable and unhealthy, unprofitable and bad for us. Until eventually the body begins to malfunction from disease, stress, and inflammation from ill-consumption and from sin abounding.

The baby is only more innocent, the child is only more innocent because sin has not yet abounded and reached its peak. Sin being *original sin* because even innocent babies and children have sin in them.

- Christ came to rescue our souls; to reconcile them back to oneness/unity with God now and in eternity.

## THESE BODIES

- Christ came to deliver our bodies from the bondage/slavery to sin while we live in THESE BODIES. He makes them, by the fruit of His Spirit, holy temples for His Presence and abode.

- The more we crucify our body and live as dead the more His being will fill us and bear all the fruits of the Spirit.

- You (or someone you know) may be hungry all the time because you are trying to fill your spiritual needs with physical substances – whether it be food, sex, drugs, alcohol, entertainment, etc.). But remember, all flesh is wholly corrupt and depraved as the penalty for sin from The Fall. So, as can be expected, there is continual harassment and demand from your body/flesh to be gratified with sinful, corrupt things because the flesh is sinful and corrupt.

- Like responds to like. Sinful flesh wants to be fed that which is sinful and indulgent and it doesn't like or want that which is not sinful and indulgent, which are the greater spiritual matter (Word of God, Bread of Life) and practices that are outside the realm of your physical senses.

APOSTLE TERRI ANDRES

## THE SUPERIORITY OF SPIRITUAL MEAT

God, who is a Spirit, takes pleasure in the sacrifice and death of flesh. Where there is no flesh, there is all spirit.

The Body of Christ, in a sense, is guilty of treason for the over-consumption of natural food (if you can even call it food as most of it is processed substances that pass for food) instead of spiritual food, bread from heaven, which is the Word, body and blood of Jesus Christ.

Because of this error, many members of the Body of Christ are weak and sick and dying premature deaths as taught in 1 Corinthians 11. We are not consuming spiritual meat by eating of the body and drinking of the blood of Christ – which translates to sacrificing our flesh in not consuming natural bread to consume spiritual bread from heaven, Christ and the Word.

*The Body of Christ must repent and then put into practice mortification of our bodily members, sinful misdeeds of the body, which include our insatiable appetites for food, drink, and entertainment.*

Receive this revelation: God needs you while you are alive in your body. To be absent from the body is to be eternally present with the Lord in spirit.

With this truth, know that, while you are alive in your body (by His breath of life), God needs you to co-labor with Him to carry out His plan for mankind and

**THESE BODIES**

the earth. Because remember, your body is what qualifies you to exist in time in this physical earth realm. Thus, in order to bring forth the Kingdom of God to earth "as it is in heaven," THESE BODIES are vital.

So, son or daughter of God the Most High, while you yet live in this world, offer your body up to God as a living, holy sacrifice which is your acceptable (keyword) and reasonable service.

*Acceptable* includes obedience in your body/members, sacrifice of your body/members and dead to practicing sin in your body/members – all of which wields the natural consequence of being alive to God (more spiritual than carnal) and thus lean in your physical stature because there is little to no fat from over-consuming natural substances.

## THE CORRUPTION OF THESE BODIES

All flesh is bad and corrupt. As the apostle Paul teaches us in Romans 7:18, there is nothing good in our flesh. This explains why it craves unhealthy and harmful substances. The condition, thus appetite, of the flesh is wholly sinful and perverse. Sinful and perverse to the extent of missing the mark of God.

Anything unlike God is sin, including us/our flesh apart from Christ.

Furthermore, when we commit sinful acts in THESE BODIES, we sin against our body which is the worst sin because sin reaps self-destruction. Romans 6:23 teaches us the fruit of sin is destruction that leads to death.

The old outward man (our flesh) is dying day by day and gets closer to death day by day, in contrast to the fruits of the Spirit that produces godliness and eternal glory in our new inner man (our spirit) day by day.

## BODILY DEATHS EXPERIENCED BY THESE BODIES

There is natural death from natural causes, unnatural death from crime and vice, and the ultimate death, which is sacrificial death for sin and for others.

## HEALING THESE BODIES THROUGH PHYSICAL DEATH

Physical death frees us from sin and suffering. Healing is freedom from sin – the effects, the consequences and the power of sin that is present, or lives, in our bodies. THESE BODIES are born in sin and shaped in iniquity. Wholly corrupt, depraved and without remedy, hence they die physically.

## GOD IN A BODY LIKE THESE BODIES

God stepped into time as a man like us and *sacrificed* His body for us. So ought we to sacrifice ours for Him.

## THE GREAT EXCHANGE IN THESE BODIES

The body of Jesus Christ, His crucified body, was made sin for our sin. The sins of our bodies. (2 Cor 5:21)

A spiritual exchange happened by spiritual imputation. We received His righteousness in exchange for our sin.

The qualification for us, believers in Him as Son of God and Savior (the Messiah), is death of our flesh. Living sacrifices. Offering up THESE BODIES as living sacrifices to then be and behave spiritual like Him- the true, acceptable worship God desires and is well pleasing to Him.

The bible teaches us that it pleased God The Father for Christ, His only begotten Son, to die in the body. The Father takes pleasure in the death of our flesh and mortification of our members. Why? So we can worship Him as spiritual sons and daughters, offering worship in spirit and in truth.

## MIND AND BEHAVIOR MATTERS OF THESE BODIES

The mind of fallen man, which is based on deception, is anti and hostile to the mind of Christ, which is based on truth. Know this: that in THESE BODIES we will never win - that is, rule and reign in Christ as God the Father intends for us to these bodies - if we continue being carnal Christians content to be and do good some of the time while willfully being and doing evil at other times and attempting to excuse our evil character and actions under God's grace.

Not only is this morally (aka spiritually) wrong, but it is also legally wrong because trust me God's grace does not cover willful sin. In fact, the bible, through the old and new covenant alike, teaches, instructs, and admonishes the exact opposite. There are many scriptures that can be cited to support this but, in particular, see the third chapter of 1 John (emphasis verse 8).

*Know this: what you do in your body is everything.*

Which is to say, every single significant action you take, nothing left out, will be profitable or detrimental. It will hurt you or help you. And because your beliefs control your thoughts and your thoughts control your actions, the belief in Christ as Son of God and Savior that brings forth a renewed and washed mind (the mind of Christ) is vital for salvation, healing, wholeness, godliness and good works produced by the fruits of the Spirit.

Therefore, we see, learn, and come into the knowledge of truth from the holy scriptures, the infallible Word of God, that we must be all of one and none of the other.

Christ says we are either for or against Him and we cannot serve God and mammon. These two things oppose each other; actually, war against each other.

## THE ANTIDOTE FOR THESE BODIES

So, what is the answer to all this that can be summed up with two big words: sin and carnality? The answer is to become spiritual sons and daughters of God. *To become spiritual like God.* For your current being (earthly existence) to transform from carnal to spiritual.

How do you become a spiritual son or a spiritual daughter? The short answer is by dying to self moment by moment. By decreasing so the Spirit of Christ can live, move and act in you.

Christ living through us, His disciples. Understand this: there are several purposes to why Christ gives us His Spirit. One of which is to overcome sin and carnality. Another is to bring others to Himself so as to rescue, heal and deliver them unto Himself and unto God the Father unto eternal life and togetherness with Him.

Further, we must understand the intention and eternal purpose of our bodies. They are *for Him.* Our bodies were made for His abode for the very purposes mentioned in the previous paragraph.

*THESE BODIES are for His dwelling and His work.*

Once again, in sum, the perfect plan of the Father is to rescue/repair/reconcile unto eternal life. To heal, set free and deliver our physical body *so that* He can work through it (not that He is not able to work through an imperfect, ill, body because He certainly can and does). The keyword is *perfect*.

> *His perfect plan is to work through His spiritual heirs, spiritual sons and daughters who have been made perfect and complete in Christ for the salvation, healing, deliverance, and reconciliation of other souls back to Himself unto eternal life in the new heaven and new earth.*

The work of the LORD is more powerful, thus more impactful, when we are holy vessels of honor unto Him without the practice of sin. The Bible in Ephesians 3:20 puts it this way: *according to the power at work within us.*

## THE CONVENTIONAL FOCUS ON ABIDING

As a maturing/mature Christian, my guess is you have heard and even seen a lot about abiding in the presence of the LORD.

From Sunday sermons to bible and small group studies, to entire books about abiding, to inspirational merchandise like mugs, pillows, and other home décor items with the *abide* message. Moreover, Jesus Himself admonishes us to abide in Him in John chapter 15.

Abiding in God is a good thing. However, I wonder, have you ever given earnest thought and consideration (that would inevitably lead you to awe, thanksgiving and praise) for God's abode in you?

## THE PROPHETIC FOCUS ON HIS ABODE IN US

Not abiding in Him, rather His abode in us. His abode in our bodies. THESE BODIES. Keep this prophetic word as the central focus while reading and receiving the rest of this message.

> *The utterly awesome reality that God the Father, master of the universe and creator of everything in heaven, in earth, and underneath the earth, has His abode in you through the Person of Holy Spirit.*

Please get this revelation and keep it at the forefront of your spiritual and natural mind for the rest of your natural life in your physical body.

Let it also be noted this revelation will be repeated throughout this book and message. Not by my own will but because the Spirit of the LORD repeated it to me as He downloaded this message.

# 4

# THESE BODIES TEACHINGS

The principal teachings that will be covered in this chapter reveal the enormous significance of physical bodies in scripture — whether it be the body of Man or the body of Jesus Christ.

As the LORD was revealing this message, I began seeing the significance of physical bodies in scripture like I had never seen before. The scriptures were illuminated. Light had come in. These teachings are what I saw in the scriptures as they relate to physical bodies.

As you read through and digest these teachings, keep this truth from 2 Corinthians 5:10 NIV at the forefront of your mind. As it is written:

> *For we must all appear before the judgment seat of Christ, so that each of us may receive what is due us for the things done while in the body, whether good or bad.*

Why the body? Why not be judged for our heart or our thoughts? There are several reasons, here are some of them. One, all physical creation, including our bodies, is under judgement and will be judged. Two, because the just (righteous in Christ) should live and walk by faith, not by sight. Three, our bodies were made for the abode of the LORD. Four, because our bodies are not our own, they belong to Christ, paid for with His blood.

And so it is, come Judgment Day, the question will be, did we use THESE BODIES for what they were meant for: good works from the abode of the Spirit of Christ in our bodies or evil bad works from the absence of His abode in our bodies?

Now make it personal. Your body? My body?

## THESE PHYSICAL BODIES

As you read and digest each of the principal teachings presented from this point forward (marked by roman numerals), keep in mind this major point: this THESE BODIES message reveals **the enormous significance of the physical body in scripture.** Whether referring to the body of a man or, moreover, referring to the body of Jesus Christ. Now, make it personal, and realize the major significance of your body to God.

## I. CIRCUMCISION

Physically, circumcision is the cutting away of flesh. Spiritually, the circumcision we have obtained in Christ is death of these corrupted bodies of sin by baptism through faith.

*"By putting off the body of the sins of the flesh, by the circumcision of Christ, buried with Him in baptism, in which you also were raised with Him through faith in the working of God, who raised Him from the dead. And you, being dead in your trespasses and the uncircumcision of your flesh, He has made alive together with Him, having forgiven you all trespasses, having wiped out the handwriting of requirements that was against us, which was contrary to us. And He has taken it out of the way, having nailed it to the cross. Having disarmed principalities and powers, He made a public spectacle of them, triumphing over them in it."*

Colossians 2:11-15 NKJV

## II. CHRIST'S BODY

The birth of Christ. The death of Christ. The resurrection of Christ. The ascension of Christ. The second coming, or Parousia, of Christ. With all of these "events" we can really put them this way: The birth of Christ's body. The death of Christ's body. The resurrection of Christ's body. The ascension of Christ's body and the second coming, or Parousia, of Christ's body.

I pray by now you are starting to clearly see the magnanimous significance of the body of Christ.

As He Himself proclaimed in Hebrews 10:5-10 (what I consider to be an epic passage of scripture, with verse 5 being the cornerstone scripture for the message of THESE BODIES), speaking to the Father, Christ says:

> "Therefore, when He came into the world, He said: 'Sacrifice and offering You did not desire, But a body You have prepared for Me. In burnt offerings and sacrifices for sin You had no pleasure. Then I said, 'Behold, I have come – In the volume of the book it is written of Me – To do Your will, O God.'" Previously saying, "Sacrifice and offering, burnt offerings, and offerings for sin You did not desire, nor had pleasure in them" (which are offered according to the law),
>
> Then He said, "Behold, I have come to do Your will, O God." He takes away the first that He may establish the second. By that will we have been sanctified through the offering of the body of Jesus Christ once for all."

## III. BAPTISM

THESE BODIES in baptism. Water baptism. The baptism of the Holy Spirit. Baptism by fire. A physical body is needed for all these baptisms. A body is water baptized. A body is baptized by the Holy Spirit – Jesus being the first of many brethren, baptized by John in the Jordan river, after which the Holy Spirit descended upon Him like a dove. A body is baptized by fire. See Matthew 3:11.

## IV. ENOCH

Just like Melchizedek, Enoch and Elijah, there will be some that never experience physical death of their body when the LORD appears again at His Second Coming. We know all these men shared a common characteristic of righteousness. That these and others will not die a physical death highlights a particular significance of our physical bodies and beckons the question how and why? How did that physically happen – physical bodies going into spiritual heaven? Why just these, and men in particular?

## V. BODIES OF SIN

These bodies of ours are bodies of sin and corruption. Inherently corrupt. Depraved. Lustful. Foul from the indwelling presence of sin. As such, apart from Christ, we are casualties and prisoners of war to our own flesh. Apart from Christ, these bodies are enslaved to sin, which make them evil, which make them enemies to the cross of Christ and enemies to our new nature in Christ.

## VI. PENALTY FOR SIN

The ultimate penalty for sin is physical death of our bodies, THESE BODIES, because of indwelling sin. And because of indwelling sin, our bodies don't work right (i.e., as God intended and designed them to work). Our flesh is totally depraved – broken, corrupt and wants whatever is sinful, again, because of the presence of indwelling sin. Sin, iniquity, and lust live in every one of us.

## VII. THE COST

The cost we must be willing to pay involves several things. One, making the Great Exchange, exchanging our life for His life so the Spirit of Christ can have permanent abode in THESE BODIES to live, move and have His being. Two, decreasing so He can increase (aka death of self). Three, total obedience to God and His Word. And four, the offering up of our bodies as living sacrifices as admonished in Romans 12:1. Read these again.

## VIII. UNION WITH CHRIST

The vitalness of this cannot be overstated. Union with Christ. Marriage to Him. Joined to Him. United with Him. One with Him. Catch this – spirit *and* body. Keyword *and*. See 1 Corinthians 6:12-20.

When we are *in Christ*, or as I like to put it, His abode in our body, we literally become a member of His body See 1 Corinthians 6:15.

THESE BODIES are joined, united, and married to Him, His Bride, the Bride of Christ (see Ephesians 5:30). This is so vital because – now really lean in to catch this – alongside reconciliation unto eternal life, union with

Christ (and each other) is God's will for mankind here on earth in THESE BODIES.

As it is written in Ephesians 1:9-10:

> 9 Making known to us the mystery of his will, according to his purpose, which he set forth in Christ 10 as a plan for the fullness of time, to unite all things in him, things in heaven and things on earth.

The book of Ephesians is one of the most popular and frequently quoted books of the bible. Endless numbers of sermons have been preached from verses and passages in this beloved Pauline epistle. But never once have I heard a cited reference to or sermon around this vital passage of scripture that so clearly reveals *"the mystery of his will and purpose"* to unite all things in Him. And not until the LORD began revealing this message to me did I myself see it.

## IX. PLACES OF WORSHIP

Old covenant physical structure tents were places of His Presence and worship of His Presence that were types and shadows of the new covenant heavenly tent (the habitation of Christ's resurrected, spiritual, glorified body) and earthly tents (the habitation of the Spirit of Christ, aka THESE BODIES), for His Presence and worship of His Presence. Under the new covenant, our bodies are holy tents/temples/sanctuaries for His dwelling. His abode in THESE BODIES.

The purification of our hearts and washing of our bodies, aka obedience, is an absolute necessity for the new covenant. See the following scripture references for evidence and further study: Ezekiel 43:1-12, emphasis on verses 10-12; Hebrews 9:13; 1 Corinthians 6:9-11; 2 Corinthians 7:1; Galatians 5:19-21; Romans 1:18-32; Colossians 3:5-10; Mark 7:15-23 and Mark 14:23.

## X. BREAD

Bread is mentioned 360 times in the King James Version of the bible. Bread is the ultimate comfort and satisfying food. Hot bread and butter. This has been the case for centuries since ancient times and is still the case today. So much that God the Father chose bread to be the thing that our LORD and Savior, His Son, is likened to – the Bread of Life.

In and under the old covenant, unleavened bread was associated with remembering the LORD and Passover (see Exodus 12:1-15).

Unleavened bread is without leaven – an agent that makes bread rise and fluffy. Yeast is the leavening agent the bible mentions and is what makes bread so satisfying. There is something about the yeast that changes the texture and complexity of the flavor. Without the yeast, you have something that resembles a thin crispy cracker.

With the new covenant, as it relates to Christ our LORD, bread represents the body of Christ and wine represents His blood. We (our spirit man) are to receive and feast on the Bread of Life, the provision of God in the Person of Christ (Rhema) and the Word (Logos).

Additionally, another important revelation about bread relates to The Sacrament of Holy Communion that includes symbols of bread and wine.

The bread represents the sinless body of Christ that was broken (sacrificed) for the redemption of our corrupted bodies of sin that, after physical death of our body and at His Second Coming, will be resurrected incorruptible spiritual bodies. The wine represents the new covenant remission of sin through the blood of Christ.

Together, the bread and wine of Holy Communion represent the sacrificial death of the sinless body of Jesus. Both are symbols of His death, which is why He admonishes us to receive them a) to remember His sacrifice and the meaning of it; and b) for us to follow suit as living sacrifices until His second coming (*Parousia*).

## XI. THE REVELATION OF THE RESURRECTION

Our bodies are promised to be, thus going to be, resurrected. The gift of the Holy Spirit is evidence of this. Acts 2:26 tells us that our flesh should dwell in hope – the anticipation of bodily resurrection. Then Acts 2:27 says the Holy One (in us) will not see decay.

## APOSTLE TERRI ANDRES

First Corinthians 15 reveals much of the mystery of the bodily resurrection. Know this: there are big, major big, plans for our bodies/bones. Can these bones live? You better believe it! But don't take my word for it, the Word teaches it. See Ezekial chapter 37 verses 1-14.

Yes THESE BODIES are for His abode in this life in time but, more abundantly, they are for resurrection into new spiritual bodies for all of eternity.

Through physical death, your body, my body, and THESE BODIES in Christ will be changed; from the old corrupt body sown and subject to decay in the grave to a new uncorrupt spiritual body resurrected by the Spirit of Christ.

In the next chapter, I will show and relate the message of these bodies in scripture. But since this all-important subject about the resurrection of our bodies can be a source of unbelief, ignorance, and confusion that lead to frustration, I feel led to include this scriptural index of proofs of bodily resurrection.

(Note all these scriptures are from the King James Version of the bible)

## 21 PROOFS OF BODILY RESURRECTION

1. Behold My hands and My feet (Luke 24:39)
2. It is I Myself, not another and a different person (Luke 24:39)
3. Handle Me, and see (Luke 24:39)

**THESE BODIES**

4. A spirit hath not <u>flesh and bones</u>, as <u>you see Me</u> have (Luke 24:39)
5. He showed them <u>His hands</u> and <u>His feet</u> (Luke 24:40; John 20:20)
6. He took fish and honeycomb and <u>did eat</u> before them (Luke 24:41-43)
7. <u>He is risen</u> (Matthew 28:6-7; Mark 16:6).
8. They <u>held Him by the feet</u> (Matthew 28:9; Luke 24:3-40)
9. They <u>saw Him</u> (Matthew 28:17; John 20:19-20)
10. They <u>found not the body</u> (Luke 24:3, 23)
11. Why seek you <u>the living among the dead</u> (Luke 24:5-6; James 2:26)
12. Jesus <u>Himself drew near</u> ... <u>He sat</u> at meat with them ... they <u>knew Him</u> (Luke 24:15, 30-31)
13. Angels said <u>He was alive</u> (Luke 24:23; Matthew 28:6-7; Mark 16:6)
14. Jesus <u>Himself stood in the midst of</u> them (Luke 24:36; John 20:19)
15. It was necessary for Christ to be crucified and to <u>rise from the dead</u> (Luke 24:46)
16. He lifted up <u>His hands</u> ... <u>He was parted from them</u>, and <u>carried into heaven</u> (Luke 24:51-52)
17. They have <u>taken away</u> the Lord out of the sepulcher [tomb] ... For as yet they knew not the Scripture, that <u>He must rise from the dead</u> (John 20:2,9)
18. Then saith he to Thomas, Reach hither thy finger, and <u>behold my hands</u>; and reach hither thy

51

hand, and thrust it into my side: and be not faithless, but believing. And Thomas answered and said unto Him, my Lord and my God. Jesus saith unto him, Thomas, because thou hast seen me, thou hast believed: blessed are they that have not seen, and yet have believed (John 20:27-29; Luke 24:37-43)

19. In all resurrections, the bodies were made alive again, not the souls. See 1 Kings 17:17-24; 2 Kings 4:18-37; 13:21; John 11 and others.
20. And one shall say unto him, What are these wounds in thine hands? Then he shall answer, Those with which I was wounded in the house of my friends (Zechariah 13:6)
21. For I delivered unto you first of all that which I also received, how that Christ died for our sins according to the scriptures; and that he as buried, and that he rose again the third day according to the scriptures (1 Corinthians 15:3-4 and the chapter in its entirety)

Resurrection life now. Keyword, *now*. Live a resurrection life *while* living in your mortal, corrupt, perishable, physical body here in time. I strongly encourage you to read and meditate on Romans 6:4-23. For your own good, knowledge, freedom, peace – whatever you need – please do not skip over this.

To end this basic teaching on *The Revelation of The Resurrection*, I'll leave you with this profound thought to ponder over. When you were physically conceived, your spirit received a natural body that grew in and birthed out of your mother's womb. Why is it so hard to believe when you physically die, your spirit will receive another body? One that is eternal and spiritual.

## XII. THE SIGNIFICANCE OF THESE BODIES

Having stated this several times now, I feel it cannot be stated and heard (read) enough – that our bodies qualify us to exist in this physical world. Our bodies are included in redemption and we will experience the fullness of this redemption through the doorway of physical death at the appointed time to die, then at the appointed time to be resurrected and receive our new spiritual bodies (know there are other events related to judgment involved as well).

Realize this: that it is our bodies and our bodies alone that are subject to physical death because of sin. Because of sin, death *must* come. As it is written in Romans chapter 8 verses 10 and 11:

> [10] *But if Christ is in you, then even though* **your body is subject to death because of sin,** *the Spirit gives life because of righteousness.* [11] *And if the Spirit of him who raised Jesus from the dead is living in you, he who raised Christ from the dead will also give life to your mortal bodies because of his Spirit who lives in you.*

Christ, Son of Man, *had* to come in the likeness of us. That is, in a body. Now is a good time to remember the anchor scripture of this entire THESE BODIES message Hebrews 10:5:

> *Therefore, when Christ came into the world, he said: "Sacrifice and offering you did not desire, but a body you prepared for me."*

Read through to verse 10 to get the full context and profoundness of this truth and how it directly applies to you – particularly the redemption of your whole self – spirit, soul, and body.

## XIII. THE SIGNIFICANCE OF CHRIST HUMAN BODY

Christ's body died for sin – all the sins of mankind (Hebrews 10:1-14). His sinless, perfect body bore our sins. It was the required sacrifice of flesh and blood (Hebrews 7:27). The righteous requirement of The Law.

As we well know now, Christ's body was crucified, resurrected, and ascended into heaven and now everlives to make intercession for us who live unto Him as living sacrifices *while* wrapped in corrupted flesh awaiting death and the fullness of new, eternal life from resurrection and glorification. Hallelujah amen!

Lastly, what I received from the LORD regarding the significance of Christ's human body is this question:

have you ever really thought about Christ's intercession for you and for others who believe in Him?

My answer was yes and the following is what the LORD said to me. *Again, this is what the LORD said to me.* I pray, in the name of Jesus, that you receive this revelation in your spirit.

*Christ is constantly interceding for God's people. What is he interceding for? Standing in place, covering our sins as our High Priest.*

Where does sin originate? In our bodies. Sin is conceived in our mind and committed through our bodies.

Still, because of the good news of the Gospel and the New Covenant, while we await glorification and new spiritual bodies, we are able to walk in the newness of life now in time through our baptism into the death of Christ (see Romans 6:1-12, with strong emphasis on verses 3-8).

Again, living sacrifices, which is how we live victorious over our flesh (the lusts of) and over all the misdeeds of our members. Amen and amen.

## XIV. COMMUNION IN THESE BODIES

Union with the body and blood of Christ. Union with the brethren, aka the household of faith, aka the Body of Christ.

Individually, we are united with Christ. Collectively, we are united, as one, to Christ *and* to each other through the Spirit of Christ.

When Christ tells us to eat of His body and drink of His blood, the underlying message is to taste death *in order that* we may taste *new* life in time and the fullness thereof in eternity.

Old versus new. Old wineskin versus new wineskin. Old, sinful nature (body) versus new righteous nature (heart and mind) through a) presenting your body as a living sacrifice; and b) the Spirit of Christ's abode in your body empowering you and producing the fruits of His Spirit in you. Old natural man vs new spiritual man.

As we just recently covered, Hebrews 10:5 reveals to us that a body was prepared for Christ (God incarnate) to be born and, moreover, to die. To die for the sins of the world in order that we might receive new, abundant life (John 10:10), which is eternal life. Catch this:

> *Real, true life is not life as you (we) know it. Real, true life is eternal life in the hereafter. A new heaven and a new earth with new glorified spiritual bodies absent of sin and death.*

This current world age as we know it is passing away in all its evil corruption. Fear, perversion and everything else. This world as we know it is not *real* life. Again (redundancy intentional), real, true, life is in Christ. Eternal life. This is one of the biggest reasons

**THESE BODIES**

Christ taught us to be not deceived. The righteous, the just, live by *faith*. What we cannot see and what we do not know with our natural reasoning. Catch this:

> *In natural order, we are born in order to die. In supernatural order, we die in order to live. Forever.*

Pause. This revelation warrants a shout of praise. Give unto the Lord your best praise aloud for as long as you feel it. HALLELUJAH!

Knowing, understanding and, therefore, receiving truth is utterly life changing. So, know this, death is not something dismal or something we should fear or dread.

> *Fear and dread of physical death is a perversion of the wonderful truth that we – our core spiritual beings – must physically depart from THESE BODIES of sin and corruption to live real, true life eternal.*

## XV. REWARD
### THE REDEMPTION OF THESE BODIES

Understand there are two rewarding aspects around the redemption of our bodies. Life in the Spirit (in time) and Future Glory (in eternity).

Note there are more scriptures than these but the following are the key scriptures the LORD gave me for this message.

57

**APOSTLE TERRI ANDRES**

## LIFE IN THE SPIRIT

Romans 8:2 - For the Law of the Spirit of life in Christ Jesus has made me free from the law of sin and death.

Romans 8:9-11 – But you are not in the flesh but in the Spirit, if indeed the Spirit of God dwells in you. Now if anyone does not have the Spirit of Christ, he is not His. And if Christ is in you, the body is dead because of sin, but the Spirit is life because of righteousness. But if the Spirit of Him who raised Jesus from the dead dwells in you, He who raised Christ from the dead will also give life to your mortal bodies through His Spirit who dwells in you.

## FUTURE GLORY

Romans 8:18-23 – For I consider that the sufferings of this present time are not worthy to be compared with the glory which shall be revealed in us. For the earnest expectation of the creation eagerly waits for the revealing of the sons of God. For the creation was subjected to futility, not willingly, but because of Him who subjected it in hope, because the creation itself also will be delivered from the bondage of corruption into the glorious liberty of the children of God. For we know that the whole creation groans and labors with birth pangs together until now. *Not only that, but we also who have the first fruits of the Spirit, even we ourselves groan within ourselves, eagerly waiting for the adoption, the redemption of our body.*

I strongly encourage you to study further by reading the entire chapter of Romans 8, as well as cross-referencing scriptures.

The key revelation to catch from this short teaching is that, in Christ (key phrase), THESE BODIES have been redeemed, in which we experience redemption to an extent now in time and will experience the full thereof in future eternity.

## XVI. THESE BODIES AND GOD'S GRACE

Where sin abounds, grace abounds much more. Because Christ's death (the death of His body) has already paid the penalty once for all.

As Hebrews 9:26b-28 states: *"but now, once at the end of the ages, He has appeared to put away sin by the sacrifice of Himself. And as it is appointed for men to die once, but after this the judgment, so Christ was offered once to bear the sins of many. To those who eagerly wait for Him He will appear a second time, apart from sin, for salvation."*

And Hebrews 9:12, *"But this Man, after He had offered one sacrifice for sins forever, sat down at the right hand of God."*

Therefore, because of the fulfillment of the Law and by paying the penalty for sin once for all, we are no longer under the law but under grace.

Further, Romans 8:2-4 states the truth of grace so clearly: *"For the law of the Spirit of life in Christ Jesus has* *made me free from the law of sin and death. For what the law could not do in that it was weak through the flesh, God did by sending His own Son in the likeness of sinful flesh, on account of sin: He condemned sin in the flesh, <u>that the righteous requirement of the law might be fulfilled in us who do not walk according to the flesh but according to the Spirit</u>."*

With this, be not deceived into believing the grace of God is a license to sin because your sins have been forgiven. This is a perverted notion and in complete error of the grace of God and the moral character of God that is holy and righteous.

As the aforementioned scripture reveals, the grace of God is for those who do not walk according to the flesh but according to the Spirit.

The works of the flesh, as written in Galatians 5:19, are evident, which are: adultery, fornication, uncleanness, lewdness, idolatry, sorcery, hatred, contentions, jealousies, outburst of wrath, selfish ambitions, dissensions, heresies, envy, murders, drunkenness, revelries, and the like.

At the risk of stating the obvious, works of the flesh are committed in the body. Think of it this way:

*Our bodies = bodies of sin = flesh = self = corrupt = lustful = evil heart = evil desires = fallen = impure = lewd = angry = idolatrous = perverse = covetous =*

*prideful = divisive = haughty = self-centered = greedy = gluttonous = every other sin.*

Through the offering up of our bodies as living sacrifices, we become like God who is a Spirit (John 4:24). Becoming a living sacrifice gives way for your spirit, being joined to His Spirit in you, to rule and reign over your flesh (body/behavior). This is *the how* to walking in the Spirit as instructed in Galatians 5:16.

Dead to sin, alive to God through the abode of His Spirit in your body ruling and reigning, living, moving, and having His way in you. Performing His good works.

## XVII. THESE BODIES BAPTIZED INTO HIS DEATH

As Christ's body died physically, so too ought we to die to practicing (keyword) sin in THESE BODIES.

Water baptism is the symbol of dying to our old sinful nature. The bible also refers to this as knowing Christ, by faith, in the baptism of His death. Christ's body died physically for our sin and our body dies figuratively *and* to the practice of sin until actual physical death when our body will physically be freed of sin. Let this sink in.

In baptism, every part of your body is immersed. Every part dies to sin and, in turn, every part rises to new life – every hurt, habit, head trip. Every childhood wound. Every offense. Every ounce of pride. Every lust. Every ill and struggle of self.

Pay special attention to the *every* and the *immersed* parts. Because only by every part (body and soul which include your mind, will, emotions, imagination, and intellect) dying to the practice of sin will we reign victorious in THESE BODIES.

## BAPTIZED INTO HIS DEATH SCRIPTURES

> Colossians 2:12 – buried with Him in baptism, in which you also were raised with Him through faith in the working of God, who raised Him from the dead.
>
> Romans 6:3 – Or do you not know that as many of us as were baptized into Christ Jesus were baptized into His death? Therefore, we were buried with Him through baptism into death, that just as Christ was raised from the dead by the glory of the Father, even so we also should walk in the newness of life.
>
> Galatians 3:27 – For as many of you as were baptized into Christ have put on Christ.
>
> 1 Corinthians 12:13 – For by one Spirit we were all baptized into one body [of Christ] – whether Jews or Greeks, whether slaves or free – and have all been made to drink into One Spirit [of Christ].

# THESE BODIES

*Acts 2:38 – Then Peter said to them, "Repent, and let every one of you be baptized in the name of Jesus Christ for the remission of sins; and you shall receive the gift of the Holy Spirit.*

Regarding Acts 2:38, the Spirit of the Lord spoke to me and said, the Body of Christ has the *repent* part down in terms of repenting to be saved. But the scripture says "repent *and* be baptized, "which is really saying – catch this – repent and DIE.

Baptism as instituted by God the Father and well-pleasing to Him, is the symbolic death of THESE BODIES of sin and corruption.

Therefore, when we claim to be in Christ, know this can be thought to mean we are literally "in" Him. We step into His death. By faith (again, until actual physical death), we die (to the practice of sin) with Him in order that we live a new resurrected, ascended life reflecting His glory (in our being) and bringing Him glory (in our good works).

## XVIII. THESE BODIES JOINED TO CHRIST

As our bodies are literally joined with Christ's crucified, resurrected, and ascended body, when we die to the flesh and live as spiritual sons and daughters born of God (who is a Spirit), by faith, we are to experience everything He did as the firstborn of many brethren.

| Christ | In Christ |
|---|---|
| His human body that died for the sins of the world | Death to the practice of sin through water baptism |
| His resurrected body that rose victorious from the grave and defeated it | Raised to new life through water baptism |
| His ascended body into heaven seated at the right hand of God ever living to make intercession of us | His Spirit's descent from heaven now living in you |

Being joined to Christ is major so please do not miss the revelation of this. And, again to over-emphasize, THESE BODIES are joined to Him through death, figuratively now by faith through water baptism and death of self/practice of sin, and literally later at His Second Coming when those who have died and are asleep will be resurrected and receive new spiritual bodies that are of one unified spirit not bound by flesh.

### JOINED TO CHRIST SCRIPTURES

*1 Corinthians 6:15, 17 – Do you not know that your bodies are members of Christ? But he who is joined to the Lord is one spirit with Him.*

*Ephesians 5:30 – For we are members of His body, of His flesh and of His bones.*

> 2 Corinthians 11:2 – *For I am jealous for you with godly jealously. For I have betrothed you to one husband, that I may present you as a chaste virgin to Christ.*
>
> Romans 7:4 – *Therefore, my brethren, you also have become dead to the law through the body of Christ, that you may be married to another – to Him who was raised from the dead, that we should bear fruit to God.*

## XIX. THESE BODIES AS END TIMES TEMPLES

This is the last principal teaching Holy Spirit gave me on this message, and how fitting for it to be eschatological in nature. In layman's terms, Eschatology is the theological study of end times.

> *THESE BODIES are the end time temples of God, being that our bodies become joined to Christ's body by His Spirit in us.*

For some reason, we don't really believe this or we partially believe it but there is still some doubt.

If this applies to you, my encouragement is to, first, pray and ask God to reveal His truth on this. Second, study the scriptures I've brought forth in the last several sections of this chapter, as well as other related new covenant scriptures. When you seek, you will find. That is Christ's promise to you (see Matthew 7:7-8).

Finally, know this, the shekinah glory of God is returning to the new temple which, collectively, is a spiritual house made up of spiritual sons and daughters that is totally unified through the presence of the Holy Spirit of God dwelling in each of us individually.

His abode in THESE BODIES. To shine the light of His glory and empower us to bear eternal fruit in the earth.

# 5

# *THESE BODIES IN SCRIPTURE*

In this critical chapter I will provide the vast scriptural evidence of the message of THESE BODIES mainly in an index format while providing context only where I feel it to be absolutely necessary.

Being this is an unabridged release, one of my chief convictions, that expectedly morphs into writing objectives, is to not add-to or take-away from how this message was given to me by Holy Spirit.

I wholeheartedly believe in the same way He revealed it to me/to my spirit, He will do the same for you.

What makes me believe this? Because the deep things of God can only be spiritually discerned by the Spirit of God. As it is written in 1 Corinthians 2:10-12

> *10 But God has revealed them to us through His Spirit. For the Spirit searches all things, yes, the deep things of God.*

> 11 For what man knows the things of a man except the spirit of the man which is in him? Even so no one knows the things of God except the Spirit of God.
>
> 12 Now we have received, not the spirit of the world, but the Spirit who is from God, that we might know the things that have been freely given to us by God.

As you read through these scriptures, I ask Holy Spirit to give you pause and open the eyes of your understanding to begin seeing the revelation of this vital message regarding our bodies and the Author of the story of life as we know it here in time, and as we hope for it in eternity with the Finisher. The Alpha and Omega. First and Last. Beginning and End. The One Who was, is, and is to come. Yahweh. Jehovah God. Our great, glorious, and good Father in heaven. I ask these things in the name of Jesus. Amen. Hallelujah!

## THESE BODIES NKJV SCRIPTURE INDEX

| | |
|---|---|
| Hebrews 10:5 | Therefore, when He came into the world, He said: "Sacrifice and offering You did not desire, But a body You have prepared for Me." |
| Hebrews 10:10 | By that we will have been sanctified through the offering of the body of Jesus Christ once for all. |
| Hebrews 10:14 | For by one offering He has perfected forever those who are being sanctified. |
| Colossians 1:22 | In the body of His flesh through death, to present you holy, and blameless, and above reproach in His sight. |
| 1 Peter 2:24 | Who Himself bore our sins in His own body on the tree, that we, having died to |

## THESE BODIES

| | |
|---|---|
| | sins, might live for righteousness – by whose stripes you were healed. |
| Romans 12:1 | I beseech you therefore, brethren, by the mercies of God, that you present your bodies a living sacrifice, holy, acceptable to God, which is your reasonable service. |
| Romans 6:6 | Knowing this, that our old man was crucified with Him, that the body of sin might be done away with, that we should no longer be slaves of sin. |
| Romans 6:11 | Likewise, you also, reckon yourselves to be dead indeed to sin, but alive to God in Christ Jesus our Lord. |
| Romans 6:12 | Therefore, do not let sin reign in your mortal body, that you should obey it in its lusts. |
| Romans 6:13 | And do not present your members [body] as instruments of unrighteousness to sin, but present yourselves to God as being alive from the dead, and your members [body] as instruments of righteousness to God. |
| Romans 7:4 | Therefore, my brethren, you also have become dead to the law through the body of Christ. |
| Romans 8:2 | For the law of the Spirit of life in Christ Jesus has made me free from the law of sin and death. |
| Romans 8:10 | And if Christ is in you, the body is dead because of sin, but the Spirit is life because of righteousness. |
| Romans 8:11 | But if the Spirit of Him who raised Jesus from the dead dwells in you, He who raised Christ from the dead will also give life to your mortal bodies through His Spirit who dwells in you. |
| Romans 8:13 | For if you live according to the flesh you will die; but if by the Spirit you put to death the deeds of the body, you will live. |
| Romans 8:23 | Not only that, but we also who have the firstfruits of the Spirit, even we ourselves groan within ourselves, eagerly waiting for the adoption, the redemption of our body. |
| Galatians 6:17 | From now on let no one trouble me, for I |

|  | |
|---|---|
|  | bear in my body the marks of the Lord Jesus. |
| Colossians 2:11 | In Him you were also circumcised with the circumcision made without hands, by putting off the body of the sins of the flesh, by the circumcision of Christ. |
| Colossians 2:12 | Buried with Him in baptism, in which you also were raised with Him through faith in the working of God, who raised Him from the dead. |
| Colossians 3:5 | Therefore, put to death your members which are on the earth. |
| 1 Corinthians 6:13 | The body is … for the Lord, and the Lord for the body. |
| 1 Corinthians 6:15 | Do you not know that your bodies are members of Christ? |
| I Corinthians 6:18 | Flee sexual immorality. Every sin that a man does is outside the body, but he who commits sexual immorality sins against his own body. |
| 1 Corinthians 6:19 | Or do you not know that your body is the temple of the Holy Spirit who is in you, whom you have from God, and you are not your own? |
| 1 Corinthians 6:20 | For you were bought with a price; therefore, glorify God in your body and in your spirit, which are God's. |
| 1 Corinthians 7:4 | The wife does not have authority over her own body, but the husband does. And likewise, the husband does not have authority over his own body, but the wife does. |
| 1 Corinthians 7:34 | There is a difference between a wife and a virgin. The unmarried woman cares about the things of the Lord, that she may be holy both in body and in spirit. |
| 1 Corinthians 9:27 | But I discipline by body and bring it into subjection, lest, when I have preached to others, I myself should become disqualified. |
| 1 Corinthians 10:16 | The cup of blessing which we bless, is it not the communion of the blood of Chrit? The bread which we break, is it not the communion of the body of Christ? |
| 1 Corinthians 11:27 | Therefore, whoever eats this bread or |

## THESE BODIES

| | |
|---|---|
| | drinks this cup of the Lord in an unworthy manner will be guilty of the body and blood of the Lord. |
| 1 Corinthians 11:28 | But let a man examine himself, and so let him eat of the bread and drink of the cup. |
| 1 Corinthians 11:29 | For he who eats and drinks in an unworthy manner eats and drinks judgment to himself, not discerning the Lord's body. |
| 1 Corinthians 11:30 | For this reason, many are weak and sick among you, and many sleep. |
| 1 Corinthians 15 | The whole chapter; emphasis on verses 17, 20-23, 35-41, 42-49, 50-56 |
| Luke 22:19 | And He took bread, gave thanks and broke it, and gave it to them, saying, "This is My body which is given for you; do this in remembrance of Me." |
| John 6 | The Bread of Life; verses 22-58 |
| Luke 11:34 | The lamp of the body is the eye. Therefore, when your eye is good, your whole body is also full of light But when your eye is bad, your body also is full of darkness. |
| Romans 1:24 | Therefore, God also gave them up to uncleanness, in the lusts of their hearts, to dishonor their bodies among themselves. |
| 2 Corinthians 4:10 | Always carrying about in the body the dying of the Lord Jesus, that the life of Jesus also may be manifested in our body. |
| 2 Corinthians 5:10 | For we all must appear before the judgment seat of Christ, that each one may receive the things done in the body, according to what he has done, whether good or bad. |
| 2 Corinthians 7:1 | Therefore, having these promises, beloved, let us cleanse ourselves from all filthiness of the flesh and spirit, perfecting holiness in the fear of God. |
| Ephesians 5:23 | For the husband is head of the wife, as also Christ is head of the church; and He is the Savior of the body. |
| Philippians 1:20 | According to my earnest expectation and hope that in nothing I shall be ashamed, but with all boldness, as always, so now also Christ will be magnified in my body, |

|  | whether by life or by death. |
|---|---|
| Philippians 3:21 | Who will transform our lowly body that it may be conformed to His glorious body, according to the working by which He is able even to subdue all things to Himself. |
| 1 Thessalonians 5:23 | Now may the God of peace Himself, sanctify you completely; and may your whole spirit, soul, and body be preserved blameless at the coming of our Lord Jesus Christ. |
| Hebrews 10:22 | Let us draw near with a true heart in full assurance of faith, having our hearts sprinkled from an evil conscience and our bodies washed with pure water. |
| James 3:2 | For we all stumble in many things. If anyone does not stumble in word, he is a perfect man, able also to bridle the whole body. |

Most of the scriptures in this index directly relate to the heart of the message of THESE BODIES – which is the offering up, sacrifice, of our bodies as the acceptable, spiritual worship God wants. Other scriptures related to our bodies are included to show the major significance of our physical bodies in scripture.

*Major significance* being the key phrase because, as pointed out in the beginning of this book, so much bible teaching today only centers around transformation of heart and mind, and only merely glosses over vital teaching about our fallen, corrupt, sin-sick bodies that the sinless body of Christ reconciles and heals. How? Through baptism into the death of His body *by faith*.

Then, Christ – His victorious, resurrected, ascended, perfect and powerful spiritual body – becomes our way of escape from our corrupted bodies by the abode of His

Holy Spirit living in us empowering us to fully obey Him and present our bodies as living sacrifices, mortifying its members, and thereby truly transforming into new creatures in Christ that are spiritual and no longer carnal possessing the evil spirit of this world. Having the mind of Christ. Having the heart of the Father aligned with His Kingdom (the Kingdom of God) set on heavenly things above and that which is eternal. Obedient to Truth, which is Christ and His Word (the Word of God). And a doer of the Word, the good works foreordained for you to do in Christ Jesus.

## SCRIPTURE INDEX NOTES

The following few notes are literal notes I added to the page margins of the scripture index in the original blue notebook when this prophetic message was being downloaded to me. I decided to include them out of obedience to Holy Spirit and I trust He will make sense of them for you and reveal what He wants to reveal to you through this THESE BODIES message.

- We are to present acceptable sacrifices to Him. Bodies that do not practice sin or sinful consumption because of out-of-control appetites. (Romans 12:1-2)
- As spiritual sons and daughters of God, we are supernaturally empowered to exist and operate in the unseen, spiritual realm by the Holy Spirit

- (the Spirit of Christ), Who lives in us to separate us from sin, snares, and temptations of the natural realm.
- For the law of the Spirit of life in Christ Jesus has made me free from the law of sin and death. (Romans 8:2)
- Christ has authority over all flesh. As He is, so are we in this world. (1 John 4:17)
- Awesome that with the tongue we are able to tame THESE BODIES.

## 10 SCRIPTURAL STATEMENTS ABOUT THE BODY

1. That the <u>body of sin</u> might be destroyed, that henceforth we should not serve sin. For he that is dead to sin is free from sin (Romans 6:6-7)
2. Who walk not after (according to) <u>the flesh</u>, but after the Spirit (Romans 8:1-4)
3. If Christ be in you <u>the body</u> is dead because of sin, but the spirit is life because of righteousness (Romans 8:10)
4. We are debtors not to <u>the flesh</u>, to live after (according to) the flesh. For it you live after the flesh, you shall die; but if you through the Spirit do mortify <u>the deeds of the body</u>, you shall live (Romans 8:12-13)
5. <u>Present your bodies</u> a living sacrifice, <u>holy</u>, <u>acceptable unto God</u>, which is your reasonable service (Romans 12:1-2)

**THESE BODIES**

6. <u>The body</u> is not for fornication, but for the Lord; and the Lord for the body (1 Corinthians 6:13)
7. <u>Your body</u> is the temple of the Holy Ghost; therefore, <u>glorify God in your body</u> and in your spirit (1 Corinthians 6:19-20)
8. Know you not that you are <u>(your body is) the temple of God</u>, and that the Spirit of God dwells in you? If any man defile <u>the temple of God (your body)</u>, him shall God destroy: for the temple of God is holy, which temple you are (1 Corinthians 3:16-17)
9. I keep under <u>my body</u> and bring it into subjection, less that by any means, when I have preached to others, I myself should be a castaway (1 Corinthians 9:27)
10. You are circumcised... without hands, in putting off <u>the body of the sins of the flesh</u> (Colossians 2:11)

These and other statements about the body and flesh emphasize the concern of God with THESE BODIES.

## 14 SCRIPTURAL FACTS ABOUT THE BODY

1. The eye is the light of the body (Matthew 6:22)
2. The body is more than meat and clothing (Matthew 6:25)
3. Both body and soul in hell (Matthew 10:28)
4. Bodies of sin (Romans 6:6)
5. Mortal bodies (Romans 6:12)
6. Mortify the deeds of the body (Romans 8:13)

7. Redemption of the body (Romans 8:23)
8. Many members of the body (Romans 12:4-5)
9. Not for fornication (1 Corinthians 6:13-18)
10. Temple of Holy Spirit (1 Corinthians 3:16; 6:19)
11. Glory God in your body (1 Corinthians 6:20)
12. Must be kept under control (1 Corinthians 9:27)
13. All acts of the body will be judged (2 Corinthians 5:10)
14. The only part of man that dies physical death (James 2:26)

## 15 SCRIPTURAL COMMANDS ABOUT THE BODY

1. Yield it to God (Romans 12:1, 6:13-20)
2. Make it a living sacrifice (Romans 12:1)
3. Make it holy (Romans 12:1; 1 Corinthians 3:17)
4. Make it acceptable to God (Romans 12:1)
5. Make it full of light (Matthew 6:22)
6. Reckon it dead to sin (Romans 6:11)
7. Reckon it alive to God (Romans 6:11)
8. Refuse its slavery to sin (Romans 6:12)
9. Mortify its deeds (Romans 8:13)
10. Refuse to defile it (1 Corinthians 3:17)
11. Make it a fit temple for Holy Spirit (1 Corinthians 3:16-17; 6:13-20)
12. Make it free from fornication and only for the Lord (1 Corinthians 6:13-20)
13. Glorify God in it (1 Corinthians 6:20)
14. Keep it in control (1 Corinthians 9:27)

15. Put off its sins (Colossians 2:11)

## THE RESURRECTED BODY IN SCRIPTURE

1. Like the present body in outward appearance (1 Corinthians 15:34-38)
2. God makes all such bodies (1 Corinthians 15:38)
3. Becomes a spiritual body (1 Corinthians 15:44)
4. Will be like Christ's body (Philippians 3:20-21)
5. Revelation of the resurrection of our bodies (Acts 2:24-28,31 AMPC; Psalm 16:10; Acts 13:16-49; Romans 6:4-23; Hebrews 2:5-18; Colossians 2:12-vital)

## THE BODY OF CHRIST

1. Made up of those (bodies) in Christ (Romans 12:5)
2. One bread and one body (1 Corinthians 10:17; Ephesians 2:16)
3. Made up of many members (1 Corinthians 12:12)
4. Men made a part of it by the Spirit (1 Corinthians 12:13; John 3:3,6)
5. The church is the Body of Christ (Ephesians 1:22-23; Colossians 1:18,22)

# 6

# *THESE BODIES CONDITION*

There are several truths to be covered on this important topic of Condition, but the one that is most profound given the overall context of the message of THESE BODIES is this one:

> *The physical condition of our body has much to do with our spiritual condition.*

Apart from medically related issues with the body, our physical condition (from our default state to misbehaviors) manifest from our unseen spiritual self that is superior to, thus rules, our physical body and behavior. On what basis? As it is written in Matthew 15:16, 19-20:

> *So Jesus said, "Are you also still without understanding? For out of the heart proceed evil thoughts, murders, adulteries, fornications, thefts, false witness, blasphemies. These are the things*

> *which defile a man, but to eat with unwashed hands does not defile a man."*

Here, Jesus is teaching us a vital truth, which is the distinction between flesh and spirit, and the superiority (or rule) of the spirit. The spiritual part of our being is what is dominant and therefore determines behavior in THESE BODIES (our flesh), which then contributes to the physical condition of them.

## FOUNDATIONAL ASPECTS OF CONDITION

Context is everything so really lean into what I am going to share here because it lays the foundation for the big ideas for *Condition*. In fact, the issues and truths about the condition of THESE BODIES is foundational to this entire prophetic message for such a time as this.

Before unpacking each of these throughout the remainder of this chapter, here is a quick summary of the key points about *Condition* that God downloaded to me:

- The condition of THESE BODIES is foundational to this prophetic message to the Bride and Body of Christ.
- Condition is not just key, but it is critical.
- When making major life decisions, you evaluate conditions.
- When purchasing something, you evaluate condition – homes, cars, any material possession, business, etc.

THESE BODIES

- Condition is another word for state.
- Our condition is determined by our:
  - Our spiritual condition
  - Our desires (passions, appetite, cravings)
  - Our mind (beliefs, thoughts, perceptions)
  - Our consumption through our bodily senses
  - Our core being (character, nobility, virtue, self-control or lack thereof, emotions, etc.)
  - Our behavior (self-disciplines or lack thereof, habits, addictions, etc.)
- Our central nervous system plays a major role in our condition. It controls so much of our physical faculties.
- The S factor - Sin:
  - Weakens our condition (makes us sick)
  - Worsens our condition (begets or brings forth more sickness and disease)
- The R Factor - Righteousness:
  - Strengthens our condition (brings healing to our default condition)
  - Betters our condition (improves our default condition. Begets wholeness, health and well-being)
- Condition and state can be used synonymously but, by default:
  - Our condition, or state, is naturally evil and corrupt

81

- Our condition, or state, causes us to behave in unhealthy and harmful ways
- Our condition, or state, betray our bodies by sickness, disease, and death. THESE BODIES hurt easily, ail easily, are fragile and fickle (just to name a few)
- Our condition, or state, is naturally evil and corrupt by default, they drive us to act evil

## WHY CONDITIONING AND STATE ARE SO IMPORTANT

We must very consciously act against our natural propensities and act opposite. If we do not oppose our evil nature, we naturally ally with it and thus ultimately destroy ourselves by way of self-sabotage and self-destructive thoughts, words, and behaviors.

If we fail to consciously decide to be good and do good – I know this is not proper English, but it gets my point across – then, by default, we will just be evil and do evil and thus experience evil outcomes.

To reiterate, our condition (or state) determines our being and behavior. We can only be good and do good if our condition is good. If our condition is bad, you guessed it, our being and behavior will be bad.

Our condition determines our moment-by-moment experiences, which determines our immediate outcomes.

Our accumulated outcomes equate to our quality of life which, largely, will be characterized by one of two things: pain or pleasure. And by pleasure I am not referring to fake, fleeting "pseudo-pleasure" (as I call it) from raw feels consumption that only work to gratify your corrupt flesh and fallen sinful nature. Rather, real, authentic pleasure from feelings of joy, fulfillment, and satisfaction in your soul and inner man. Your spirit. Zoë, the Breath of Life, God, inside of you.

### CORRECTING OUR CONDITION: SPIRITUAL TRANSFORMATION BY THE POWER OF GOD

In conclusion to this opening summary, do you see how your condition determines whether your overall experience in your being and life will be good and blessed or bad and sad?

Read the above statement again and really take it in because it is saying a lot – which is the very reason why *Condition* is foundational to this entire message.

So, what's the remedy? We will take a deep dive into *Remedy* in the next chapter but, essentially, to get and stay on the right course, we need the power of God that comes through spiritual awakening and spiritual transformation into His sons and daughters made in His image and likeness, possessing His heart, mind, and character/attributes so we can be and, in turn, behave like Him.

Let's now get into unpacking all of this, shall we?

APOSTLE TERRI ANDRES

## THESE BODIES CONDITION BY DEFAULT

Cutting right to the chase, the default (keyword) condition of all our bodies is corrupt because of the presence of sin. As it is written in Psalm 51 and verse 5:

*Behold, I was brought forth in iniquity, and in sin my mother conceived me.*

So, when you refer to your body, you can really refer to it as "my body of corruption." Now, I understand this may be a harsh thing to hear, but every bit of it is true as taught extensively and clearly in the Word of God. I am just the messenger here.

With the exception of one being/body, Jesus Christ as Son of Man, every human body born is corrupt in our core. Which, I understand is contrary to what you may have been taught to the tone of being a good person that does good works. This is a hard pill to swallow, I know.

Nevertheless, because we have the potential to carry out evil (*potential* being the keyword), our very nature is evil and corrupt and this corruption is carried out exclusively in the body. Hence the biblical phrase "bodies of sin."

On the other hand, there is our spirit. No physical body, no iniquity, no sin, no misdeeds, no corruption.

*THESE BODIES are the issue and our way of escape is spiritual transformation.*

**THESE BODIES**

To, here in time, mature from carnal to spiritual until full liberation and glorification forever in eternity through the doorway of physical death. Hallelujah amen! This is most definitely something to give shouts of praise to God for and something to look forward to.

:: BRIEF INTERMISSION ::

Son or daughter of God, whose name is Yahweh, please do not be disheartened by the abrasive truths presented here and throughout this message. The bible teaches us in Hosea 4:6, God's people are destroyed for lack of knowledge. Therefore, knowledge – *right* knowledge – is power and when you know better you do better. You believe better, think better, speak better, and thus behave better. Knowing the default condition of your body as corrupt due to its very nature, empowers you to think and act in ways that lead to divine healing and wholeness.

## THESE BODIES CONDITION BY CONSUMPTION

The good news is, even though the default condition of our bodies is and will always be corrupt, we are able to affect – whether positively or negatively – our physical condition through our consumption. Catch this:

*What we consistently consume contributes to our physical condition. How we feel and function.*

This means, to significant degrees, our physical condition is further determined by what we consistently consume through our bodies – specifically, through our physical senses of sight, sound, touch, and taste (not so much smell, however this can apply in a narrow context in terms of a sexual fetish that turns into addiction).

Whether your overall physical condition is excellent, fair, or outright poor as determined by 1) how well you physically feel; 2) how well you physically function; and 3) your level of physical resiliency when life hits hard.

## THESE BODIES CONDITION BY CONDITIONING

Consumption in the context above is like the saying "you are what you eat", which is very true. But know this, what you consistently consume goes beyond determining your condition in terms of outcome (how you feel, function etc.). Conditioning is at play. Which is to say, what you consistently consume quite literally *makes* up your condition.

What you consistently consume make up the matter of your mind/thoughts which, in turn, make up the words you speak which, in turn, make up the actions you take (which become habits and/or addictions depending on if the habit is healthy or unhealthy), which altogether determine your outcome – what you experience from one moment to the next which amount to the overall quality, or condition, of your life. All stemming from the way you've conditioned your body from consumption we take in and, in turn, behaviors we act out. Pretty deep. Let it sink in.

## THESE BODIES CONDITION AND DIVINE INTENTION

One day sitting in my car during a lunch break, as I was observing men and women pass by, Holy Spirit started speaking this to me. The revelation that the body of Man is Elohim's (the plural name of God as Creator) highest creation. That human beings in human bodies are a phenomenal wonder to be marveled over.

I pondered at length and spoke these words to God. *Your intention, Elohim, was that we would operate a little lower than angels in THESE BODIES. That we would be intelligent creative beings in the very likeness of You. That the body is just a tent – a marvelous tent but a tent nonetheless – that housed intelligent creative beings that were far superior and dominated all other created beings.*

*Yet we are operating at such dumb and debase places in THESE BODIES excessively consuming and coveting some sort of digital content.*

*You had in mind that we would create and that we would accomplish great exploits. But we are not doing any of that. We are not living the vision you intended for us. We are not living as gods. As your highest creation crowned with glory and honor. Because we are constantly* consuming and feeding the lower corrupt nature of our triune being, our flesh.

Everything that can be consumed, we are overconsuming and, subsequently, mentally conceiving, thus acting out all kinds of lewd behaviors in THESE BODIES.

Which, of course, begets corruption that is breeding and reaping corruptions in THESE BODIES such as cancers, type 2 diabetes, heart disease, and other chronic mental and emotional illnesses that are taking us out prematurely, and therefore keeping us from operating at the high heavenly level we were designed to operate because of the consequences that come from feeding corruption. Lacking the zeal of the Lord due to THESE BODIES not feeling well and not functioning optimally. Hormonal imbalances. Brain fog. Fatigue. Frustration. Sleep deprivation and poor diets due to the busy pace of our self-centered lives that are ensnared in modern day digital and social media culture.

Another inspired thought I had about the bodies of men being made magnificent in the image and likeness of God, was of ancient Greeks and their fixation on the human body. While their philosophy was not aligned with Christ-centered doctrine, they regarded the human body as a temple, as sacred and worthy of high praise to the point of deifying it.

> Why are we, humanity, the heart/mind and soul of man, missing the mark so much on this?

## THESE BODIES

> *Why are we not in a relentless, high pursuit for our spirits to exist in sacred, holy temples acceptable to our Creator?*

Because of the bad and sad condition of our beings in THESE BODIES -- spirit, soul, and body. Increasing in corruption because of evil worldly deceptions, temptations, distractions, and evil consumption that determines our appetites and continuous cravings for all of these things.

And into the *Cycle of Corruption* (as I've coined it) we go. Spiraling downward, out-of-control until hitting rock bottom.

Take technology and social media, for example. How it has men, women, young adults, and teenagers addicted to screens and bound in gross ways.

Further, the covetousness, social comparison, lures and temptations, identity issues, unhealthy obsessions with likes in lieu of true love and connection. Self-esteem issues and the list of ills, unfortunately, goes on and on.

> *Remember, we become (spiritually and physically) what we consume and our consumption determines our thoughts, ideas, appetites, and cravings which, in turn, determine our actions and outcomes.*

# 7

# *THESE BODIES REMEDY*

Now then, having more knowledge and understanding from the previous chapter about the physical condition of THESE BODIES, the imperative question that begs to be addressed at this point center around the remedy for the physical condition of THESE BODIES which is, by default, naturally inherently corrupt and abounds in corruption by our willful consumption and behavior.

## THE BIGGEST THING NEEDED

Before sharing the biggest thing needed, let me first share that the meaning of "remedy" always refers to a partial remedy. Keyword, *partial*. Because as long as our spirits are housed in these wonky, broken, sin-sick, fleshly bodies of corruption, we can only experience a foretaste of the full and final glory that is to come – that is, the glorification of THESE BODIES when Christ our Savior returns for us at His second coming, the *Parousia*.

With this being understood, the biggest thing needed to remedy our condition is this:

> *We need transformation from carnal beings to spiritual beings. To transform into spiritual sons and daughters of God that have been born of His Spirit.*

To be frank, a *spiritual* house (keyword *spiritual*) is the one and only household Christ is coming back for, and this is by far the biggest thing we need in terms of remedy for the inherently corrupt physical condition of THESE BODIES. To become *spiritual* sons and daughters. Read and meditate on 1 Corinthians 3:1-3.

## CONDITION AND THESE BODIES

For the sake of clarity, while *condition* includes our spiritual condition, primarily, references are to the condition of our physical bodies – their condition by default (due to indwelling sin) and their condition by consumption and actions – which these truths and more were just covered in the previous chapter *Condition*. If you have not yet read this chapter, go back and read it first in order to fully understand this chapter on *Remedy*.

## SPIRIT STRONG IN THESE BODIES

Let me start by again stating, the only true, acceptable worship to God is what we do in THESE BODIES as spiritual sons and daughters. Spiritual beings that beget

**THESE BODIES**

spiritual behavior. To put it short and sweet, there are two parts to "spiritual behavior": a) you presenting your body as a living sacrifice, dead to self with mortified members, which allows for; b) the Spirit of Christ living, moving, and having His being in you.

This is where spiritual strength comes into play.

*To be spirit strong is to be spiritual. To be more like God. The more spiritual you are the more like God you are because God is not only a Spirit, He IS Spirit.*

A holy Spirit set apart from, above and ruler over everything. Meditate on this to allow it to sink in.

As for you and your transformation into a spiritual son or daughter born of God, to be spirit strong is to be ruled by your inner man. To be (exist) like Him in likeness (character) and deeds (good works.)

As spiritual sons and daughters (heirs) of God in Christ Jesus, from a natural perspective, as oxymoronic as it may sound, our overarching goal while living in THESE BODIES is to be and live spirit strong.

*For your spirit-man to be stronger than your natural-man and thereby enabling you to be and behave spiritually. Living from your spirit by the power of Holy Spirit.*

Remember, it is our inner spirit-man that becomes joined to the Spirit of God – which is why the bible teaches and instructs us to move from babes in Christ to mature adults in Him. This maturation is the process of spiritual transformation. First, born of water (natural man), then born again of God (enlivened spirit-man).

The *what, when, where, why,* and *how* to become Spirit Strong™ is an in-depth teaching I have separate from this message, but suffice it to say here, the only true and acceptable worship to God is what we do in THESE BODIES as spiritual beings. Spiritual sons and daughters behaving spiritually. The Spirit of Christ increasing more and more to strengthen our spirit and self decreasing more and more to weaken and deaden our flesh. Which results in slaves to righteousness, no longer slaves to self, sin, and unrighteousness.

## THE KEY TO OVERCOMING STRUGGLES WITH SELF

Catch this. Naturally, you can't just stop one thing and not have something else to replace it with.

Something that is more satisfying, or better said something that is more noble and more virtuous. Something that is like the character of God. Something that is good.

After all, you are made in His image and *likeness*, so to do something *like Him* Who is good (versus evil) and full of virtue is what's needed.

On what basis do I suggest this? Because, foundationally, there is a dichotomy to life.

Deity, Man. Good, Evil. Law, Grace. Spirit, Flesh. Supernatural, Natural. Man, Woman. Hot, Cold. Black, White. Happy, Sad. And everything else big and small.

Therefore, when trying to end some evil, we need to replace it with good. The bible teaches us in Romans 12:21 to overcome evil with good. This is the key.

## THE STEPPING STONES OF SPIRITUAL TRANSFORMATION

The way to bring about this transformation is first through awareness, then desire, then will, then reconditioning.

As a sidebar, before diving into these, I used 'stepping stones' versus 'steps' to title this section because, while the inherent meaning of steps does carry chronological order, there are occasions where steps can be executed out-of-order and one can still ultimately reach success.

But the idea of stepping stones is different. Stepping stones are used to cross over something in order to get to something else and each step is necessary.

For spiritual transformation, you will never get here without awareness, then desire, then will, and last reconditioning – in this order.

### 1.AWARENESS

Awareness is the absolute essential for transformation. All transformation starts here because awareness is knowledge. Knowledge and understanding that something exists or is happening (past, present, future). The bible teaches us in Proverbs 4:7 that, along with wisdom, the getting of knowledge and understanding is the principal thing. Keyword, *principal*.

## 2. DESIRE

After awareness is desire. There must be desire and what determines desire is what is in your heart. We must have a change of heart. We must want what God wants in our heart. We must want to obey Him with all our heart.

When something is in our heart, very little if anything will stop you from going after and getting the desire of your heart. In fact, you will not stop until you obtain the object of your desire.

When we have a change of heart, then we are in position to recondition. Catch that. When we have a change of heart, then we are in position to recondition. Our hearts need a complete Christ takeover and makeover. Let me say this again louder for the people in the back. Our hearts need a complete Christ takeover and makeover.

## 3. WILL

LORD, not as I will but Thy will be done. This will need to be your utmost decision and declaration if you are to transform into a spiritual son or daughter born of God, born of His Spirit.

*Will* translates to death of self. It is the surrendering of your God-given free will back to Him. Humbling and emptying yourself of pride and ego. Decreasing, or dying to self, that the Spirit of God can increase (live, move and have His being in you).

### 4. RECONDITIONING

Reconditioning is a process that happens through death of self (denying oneself and guarding your gates of the stuff you need to get rid of) and, in turn, consuming the right things – the Word and other spiritual meat, spiritual disciplines and spiritual practices.

This thought of reconditioning came as I was listening and had been listening to classical music while I worked (in obedience to the Word to make the most of every opportunity and show myself approved) on this book versus idle entertainment on social media or streaming worldly content. Reconditioning is one of the necessary components to becoming spirit strong. Reconditioning is a deliberate and intentional process. It will require conviction, decision, commitment, and consistency.

## DIALING BACK CONSUMPTION IN THESE BODIES

With THESE BODIES of ours, it is largely our consumption that really gets us into trouble. What we are consuming through our eye and ear gateways, as well as through our taste and intimacy, which include food and drink consumption and sexual activity.

Dialing back your consumption goes a long, long way because most of what we consume is evil consumption which causes sin to abound and ultimately bring forth death.

*When you stop consuming you, in effect, stop sinning.*

Obviously, this statement does not apply to sinful actions or behavior. The context is consumption and in this vein, rather than sin having constant chances to abound through whatever consumption (feeding), the sin that lives in THESE BODIES of corrupted flesh begins to starve to death.

*Consequently, we grow spiritually. We become spirit strong as our flesh weakens.*

If you are having a struggle in one area, I am willing to bet there is some area that you are strong in. So instead of focusing on trying to completely stop consumption in your area of struggle, dial back consumption in another area and be consistent.

*Over the course of time, as you grow spiritually, you will be stronger and able to overcome in that other area or areas of struggle.*

## FALLING SHORT:
## NOT IF BUT WHEN AND WHAT TO DO ABOUT IT

As Jesus taught His disciples then and us today, "the spirit indeed is willing but the flesh is weak."

Even when we grow from being carnal babes in Christ to being mature spiritual sons and daughters, we will fall short, not just of His glory (according to Romans 3:23), but also fall short of doing what we will and ought to do, and instead do what we do not necessarily want to do but are weak and powerless over whatever that something is. Classic, age-old good versus evil behavior.

Why is this? In a word, weakness.

*Naturally and spiritually we are weak.*

As I have already expounded upon greatly throughout this text, THESE BODIES are bodies of sin and corruption. Something that is corrupt is naturally weak.

Spiritually we are weak, by and large, because of our consumption. We are a) carnal and worldly and b) surviving on natural bread alone; instead of c) living holy set apart from the world and d) feasting daily on the Word of God as bread. Keyword, *feasting*. Not merely tasting, but feasting. Big difference!

So how do you become strong – in body and spirit? The answer is deciding on c and d. Admittedly, easier said than done but 100% possible in Christ.

As it is written in Matthew chapter 19 verse 26:

> *But Jesus looked at them and said to them, "with men, this is impossible but with God all things are possible."*

## TRANSFORMATION: BECOMING BEING AND BEHAVING SPIRITUAL

Okay, lean in close because what I share in this section really needs to get deep in your spirit, your core being and consciousness. So read it then study it then read it and study it and keep studying it until it is revelation knowledge beyond mere head knowledge.

Essentially, there are two parts to the necessary transformation that remedy our physical condition, thus experience in THESE BODIES.

Part 1: The offering of spiritual sacrifices (which inherent to this is obedience, or the other way around, inherent to obedience is the offering of spiritual sacrifices unto God). With this, what must always be remembered and practiced is John 4:24, a vital truth and instruction for the Bride and Body of Christ: God is a Spirit and they that worship Him must worship Him in spirit and in truth.

> *Too prevalent today with the perversion of the Gospel is this casual Christian aura that is completely absent of the fear of God.*

As such, we just "throw out" (pun intended) scriptures and quote them so casually that we discount the most profound aspect of them – that they are living, breathing and active. Did you catch that? Living, breathing and active. God and His Word are one and the same. There is no separation between the two.

Within the frame of this vital context, we ought to be offering spiritual sacrifices unto God – the only ones that are acceptable to Him.

Spiritual sacrifices are sacrifices of praise, thanksgiving, singing to the LORD a new song, presenting your body as a living sacrifice, and operating in this world, willfully and noticeably different, as a citizen of heaven. All of which require humility, the removal of pride and self in relation and submission to the Godhead.

Part 2: When part one is in play, the Spirit of Jesus Christ is now able to live, move and have His way in you. To increase in you as you have decreased (humbled yourself and fully surrendered your will for His).

## THE CORE FOUR IN THESE BODIES

I want to emphasize and will keep emphasizing, what I refer to as "The Core Four," which are governing tenets for born-again believers in Christ to live by.

Primarily, God the Father is looking for from us: 1) belief in Him and His Son, Jesus, as Messiah, Savior and LORD; 2) obedience to His Word/Truth; 3) spiritual sacrifices offered to Him; and 4) good works that He predestined us to do before the foundation of the world.

## 1. BELIEF IN HIM

This is ground zero. The starting point for any and everything that relates to salvation and redemption through the finished work of Jesus Christ.

You must a) believe God is who He says He is through His Word written (logos) and spoken (rhema); and b) believe Jesus is the Son of God, promised Messiah, and Savior of the world unto eternal life.

As it is written in Hebrews 11:6, *"But without faith, it is impossible to please Him, for he that cometh to God must believe that He is and that He is a rewarder of those who diligently seek Him."*

## 2. OBEDIENCE TO HIM

Obedience to Him is obedience to His Word, which is the same as saying obedience to Truth because God is His Word and He is Truth. There is no separating God from His Word or from the truths of His Word, which is why the bible is referenced as the Word of Truth. Truth is also one of His proper names.

After belief in Him, *full* obedience is an absolute must. Period. Without obedience, your being, body, and behavior are rebellious, making you against God. Making you an enemy of God instead of His child.

As it is written in Matthew 12:30, Christ said, *"He who is not with Me is against me, and he who does not gather with Me scatters abroad."*

True children of God are fully obedient. Keyword, *fully*. So, understand well that obedience and rebellion are the only two locus and they are opposite positions. From God's view, the portrait and characterization of your being and life will be obedience or rebellion. One or the other. This is black and white with zero grey in this matter.

Besides being ubiquitous throughout the entire canon of scripture, the call to obedience is clear and comprehensible for all. No theological exegesis needed. Obedience is as basic as belief in Him and this is His intentional design.

### 3. SPIRITUAL SACRIFICES

Spiritual sacrifices are: belief, faith, trust, hope, obedience, the offering of your body as a living sacrifice, worship, prayer, praise, thanksgiving, and virtuous exchanges such as humility instead of pride, unity instead of division, love instead of fear, hatred and war, wise instead of foolish, contentment instead of covetousness, self-restraint instead of lust, pure instead of polluted, giver instead of taker, peace instead of worry, calm instead of rage, cheerful instead of depressed, zealous instead of lazy, creative instead of consumer, others-centered instead of self-centered, and so on.

When it comes to sacrifices of praise – a noteworthy spiritual sacrifice in that, over and over throughout the Word of God – we are admonished to give unto God incessantly, without ceasing. I have written an entire book (that will be released after this one) about why this is so, but the bottom line is because always praising God removes any and everything evil from the equation.

Further to understand about praise is this: that our old nature will naturally sing the old. Old sad songs of fear, anger, resentment, worry, anxiety, depression, frustration, etc., over what did or did not happen to us (past tense) and/or what is or is not happening to us (present tense).

On the other hand, our new nature in Christ can sing nothing but a victory song. Our new song in Christ is only a victory song. As it is written in 1 Corinthians 15:57, "but thanks be to God, who gives us the victory through our Lord Jesus Christ."

The ability to offer sacrifices of praise without ceasing – regardless of your mental, emotional, or physical state; regardless the situation or circumstance – depends upon you being a new (spiritual) creature in Christ. One who has been born of God, born of the Spirit and now uses your body as His abode. This makes spiritual transformation into a spiritual son or daughter, Christ being the firstborn, imperative.

Read this section repeatedly until you really understand it and receive the truth of it in your spirit.

**THESE BODIES**

### 4.GOOD WORKS

As it is written in Ephesians 2:10, *"for we are his workmanship, created in Christ Jesus for good works, which God prepared beforehand that we should walk in them."*

God's nature is good, as was all of Creation before the Fall (the event that made man and everything made evil). As a part of God's magnificent plan of redemption that is unfolding from one moment to the next, we, the Body of Christ, are God's workers of good in this world.

If you are truly in Christ, wholly surrendered and fully obedient, there are unique, specific, drawn-out plans of good works for you to carry out for the building of the Kingdom of God, which is an everlasting, spiritual Kingdom made up of spiritual sons and daughters with the risen and ascended Christ as the firstborn.

In closing this *Core Four* section, as I stated in the opening paragraph, these are monumental governing tenets you should be aware of, understand and, in turn, apply. Earnestly study them so you can walk them out.

## DECISIONS YOU GET TO MAKE

Honestly, it is not impossible to consistently do what is right and good for THESE BODIES. It does, however, require the giving over of oneself in the forms of self-sacrifice, self-control, self-denial, and self-discipline.

I refer to this as The Great Exchange and, while not easy, it is attainable when you want it. When your deepest heart's desire is to become (transform), be (exist) and behave (operate) as your heavenly Maker and Father intended for you. As His spiritual son or spiritual daughter, born of Him with His nature, His character attributes, and His actions.

The payoff is exponentially greater than the fleeting, momentary quick fix you get from a raw feel, which is whatever makes you feel good regardless of its ultimate negative, or more accurately described evil, effects and/or consequences.

But here's what I really want you to catch as a concluding thought as it relates to the remedy for the condition of THESE BODIES of ours:

*Decision comes before self-discipline and self-control.*

When you get to the point of wanting what God wants for you *more than* what you want for yourself (no matter how big or small) from your moment-by-moment decisions to major decisions for yourself, family, and life affairs, you must first make a hardline, uncompromising decision.

In short, your decisions stem from the desires of your heart. So having the heart of God is the golden key. After this, your decisions begin to align with His Word of

Truth, full of commands and admonishments for your total good.

Practically, your decisions are your commitments. Your covenants, or agreements, with yourself.

Strategically, your decisions determine how you show up moment-by-moment for yourself and how you respond to people, things, situations, and circumstances outside of yourself.

Lastly, remember this and recall it often: life always presents us with the opportunity to choose. To choose what is good and right or choose evil and wrong.

# 8

# *THESE BODIES AND OUR WORSHIP*

What does the acceptable worship God wants in THESE BODIES look like? The keyword here being *acceptable*.

In chapter one, *God Wants Your Body*, I provided a pretty decent summary of acceptable worship. Here, I will provide the depth to acceptable worship – what it is; what it is not; what it looks like; and how to offer it. All of which is based on the words of our LORD found in the fourth chapter of Saint John, for it is Christ Himself Who gives us the answer.

But before I go any further, to prepare your heart more to receive these truths, I ask that you pause and really marvel at this, the fact that this is what Christ, God incarnate, says to us about the worship He wants.

Are you ready to receive His truth?

As it is written in the gospel according to Saint John chapter 4 verses 21-24:

> *21 Jesus said to her, "Woman, believe Me, the hour is coming when you will neither on this mountain, nor in Jerusalem, worship the Father.*
>
> *22 You worship what you do not know; we know what we worship, for salvation is of the Jews.*
>
> *23 But the hour is coming, and now is, when the true worshipers will worship the Father in spirit and truth; for the Father is seeking such to worship Him.*
>
> *24 God is Spirit, and those who worship Him must worship in spirit and truth.*

Acceptable worship manifests itself in various forms, which I will cover, but basically this is it; that the two fundamentals to acceptable worship to God in THESE BODIES are: 1) in spirit; and 2) in truth.

## HOLY WORSHIP

God is holy and because of this any worship offered to Him and acceptable by Him must be holy. Do we not see example after example of this in His Word? Offerings that had to be set apart in some way, along with the shedding of blood – which is the byproduct of the sacrifice/death that flesh offerings to God require.

Really hear me and receive the following revelation:

**THESE BODIES**

*Any and all flesh has to be sacrificed unto death because God is Spirit and they that worship Him must worship Him in spirit and in truth.*

The worship offerings of old under the Law were types and shadows of the new and better worship that would be offered under Grace – holy spiritual offerings absent of the sin and/or corruption inherent to flesh.

As a born-again child of God in Christ, as long as you live in bodily form, your sinful flesh must be sacrificed to worship. Once sacrificed, then you are in the right state to worship God in a way that is acceptable to Him.

Always remember, holy (spirit) cannot mix with unholy (flesh). As it is written in John chapter 3:

> [5] *Jesus answered, "Most assuredly, I say to you, unless one is born of water and the Spirit, he cannot enter the kingdom of God.* [6] *That which is born of the flesh is flesh, and that which is born of the Spirit is spirit.* [7] *Do not marvel that I said to you, "You must be born again."*

Holy worship in THESE BODIES practically involve three basic things: 1) wholly dying to self; 2) wholly turning away from the world; and 3) wholly turning to God. Inherent in these are 1) belief in God; 2) obedience to Him; 3) thanksgiving and praise; and 4) good works. I refer to these as "The Core Four."

APOSTLE TERRI ANDRES

## CORRECTING FALSE FORMS OF WORSHIP

By now it should be clear what true acceptable worship to God is. However, the picture of worship that comes to mind for most Christians are praise and worship sessions in Christian gatherings. Clapping, hand-raising, singing (including hymns that characterize quieter congregations versus charismatic ones), dancing, bending knees, bowing over, shouts of praise and the like.

Moreover, and sadly so, beyond a mere picture, this is the reality and form of worship offered by so many well-meaning Christians who love God and from this love want to worship Him with every fiber of their being.

This man-made form of worship stems from religion with all its denominations and traditions, from ancient times throughout generations to now. And, as well-meaning as it may be, it is not the worship God wants, nor is it acceptable to Him. You may argue, God looks at the heart, to which my response would be, yes He absolutely does. However, this is only one measurement of judgment. Children of God are commanded and admonished throughout the full canon of scripture, but particularly, in the New Covenant, to be and behave like children of God. To always pray, to always give thanks, to present your body as a living sacrifice, to mortify your members, to come out of the world, to abstain from sexual immorality, to stay away from the appearance of evil, to grow in the grace and knowledge of God (which involves studying to show thyself approved and able to rightly divide the Word of God), and so on. This is just to name a few from a very long list of commandments and admonishments. Non-adherence, which is a nice way to put disobedience, is an insult to the Spirit of grace. As it is written in Hebrews 10:26-31:

> *26 For if we sin willfully after we have received the knowledge of the truth, there no longer remains a sacrifice for sins,*
>
> *27 but a certain fearful expectation of judgment, and fiery indignation which will devour the adversaries.*
>
> *28 Anyone who has rejected Moses' law dies without mercy on the testimony of two or three witnesses.*
>
> *29 Of how much worse punishment, do you suppose, will he be thought worthy who has trampled the Son of God underfoot, counted the blood of the covenant by which he was sanctified a common thing, and insulted the Spirit of grace?*
>
> *30 For we know Him who said, "Vengeance is Mine, I will repay," says the Lord. And again, "The LORD will judge His people."*
>
> *31 It is a fearful thing to fall into the hands of the living God.*

Sure, you would be judged innocent if you never had the opportunity to learn the truth. Personally, I believe these cases will be few and far between because, respectfully, most Christians today are carnal, worldly, disobedient idolaters. In different seasons of my new life and walk with Christ, these unfortunately rang true for me as well.

If the shoe fits, don't feel bad to the point of condemnation and shame. But do repent. Change your mind, change your direction. Now that you are learning what true worship is, humbly receive it with gladness and allow it to change your heart. It absolutely will. How can I be so sure? Because this is God's will for you!

## A RAW PICTURE OF TRUE WORSHIP

I debated whether I would include the following greyed-out section. It is in its raw form from when the Spirit of the LORD inspired me to utter it. Immediately, as I always do, I recorded myself while speaking then later converted it to text from voice. I decided to include it because I believe someone reading this may only be able to catch exactly what they need from it in this raw form. Note I purposely did not edit this, so it is full of grammatical and syntax errors.

> *True acceptable worship is spiritual worship, the offering of spiritual sacrifices unto God, full belief in him fear of him. We got a lot of fears. We got fears*

**THESE BODIES**

*of man fears of going without fears of the unknown fear of being sick, and a lot of fears related to self, and living in this world, and in the spirit of this world, but we lack fear of God true worship is spiritual worship. In this fear of God. True worship is the offering of your body as a living sacrifice. True worship is full obedience to the word of God, and not rebellious rebellion, true obedience is sanctified, set apart, living from set apart from this world, living separated from the spirit of this world, true worship is full obedience to the father full worship is not being an idolator and not coveting things and not having selfish ambition and having self-control, and having love and not offense, this is true worship and spirit, and in truth, True is worship and spirit is walking in the spirit and not walking in the flesh. It's being a spiritual son and daughter, and not a carnal Christian. this is true worship. It is not on Sundays in the church building with your hands lifted with your eyes, looking up into heaven and singing and clapping and going into this " spiritual flow. This is not true worship that is acceptable to God is worship and spirit, and in truth, and that truth part is exulting his truth it is singing of praise, and Thanksgiving incessantly no matter what's going on with you or around you no matter what happened to your loved one no matter what's happening to you no matter what's happening in the world, but always giving thanks to*

*God singing soul and praise, singing a new song regardless, in the good and the bad that is true worship in Jesus name amen. We've got the change the picture that we have in our mind of what worshiping God is, it is the offering of yourself. It is the offering of your whole entire self: spirit, soul, and body. Don't forget the body part. And if the offering of your whole entire being, the totality of your being to God for him to live, move and have his being in you to be a holy sanctified, set apart from sin vessel, so he can live in you moving you and work through you in Jesus name. This is the picture, but it is not just a picture. This is the reality of true acceptable worship. When we get the picture and the reality of worship don't change our worship it will change our selves. Hallelujah will transform us into the spiritual sons and daughters of God, born of God and born of his spirit and become the spiritual house. The bride and body of Christ is a spiritual house and this is the house that he is coming back for in Jesus name hallelujah amen. Know this and live with it in mind. Christ is coming back to judge his people in righteousness and in truth. Key phrase in truth. Which is another reason worship of Him must be in truth – aside from the biggest reason we worship God in truth, which is because he himself is truth. So in this context, worshiping him in truth is the only way we can truly worship him.*

## WORSHIPING GOD AS HIS BRIDE

This is another important picture of worshipping God in spirit. A picture that, as a child of God (which, again, for the umpteenth time, means you are spiritual and not carnal or you are still a babe in Christ in the process of maturing to this), you need to see and keep at the forefront of your mind.

I believe for most reading this, you are well-informed on being the Body of Christ but I am not as sure about the Bride of Christ. So, let me ask you: how much weight do you place on being the Bride of Christ? By weight I mean, how much does knowledge of this influence and control your worship?

A keyword in my last question is *knowledge*. You must have knowledge on what the Bride of Christ truly is in order to identify and establish (through your heart/mind, desire, decisions, convictions, commitments, etc.) yourself as His bride.

Here is a wonderful picture of the Bridegroom and His Bride in conversational story form between a teacher and his student:

> *"BEHOLD THE CALLAH," said the teacher, as he drew my attention to a young woman in the tent village. "It's how you say 'the bride' in Hebrew. Do you remember when the bridegroom made his visit? It was for her."*

"And yet she's still here," I said, "She's the bride but not yet married."

"In the Hebrew wedding, the bridegroom journeys to the house of the bride. There in that house, or tent, the covenant is made. They are from that moment on considered bride and groom, husband and wife. But the bridegroom must then leave the bride and her house and journey back to where he came from. The two are joined in the covenant of marriage. But they don't see each other until the day of the wedding. They spend their time preparing for that day."

But for the bride, it seems as if nothing's changed. She still lives with her family in that tent. She's still doing her daily chores. Her surroundings are the same. Her life is the same. She's married, but what's changed?

"She's changed," he said. "She is now the calah!"

"I don't understand."

"Two thousand years ago the Bridegroom journeyed to the house of the bride, God journeyed to this world, to our house, to our lives. And, likewise, it was to make a covenant. According to the mystery, the bridegroom must leave the bride's house and return home. So Messiah then left this world to return to heaven. So these now are the days of the separation. *The Groom is in His house, heaven. And we, as the bride, are in our house, this world. And if you've said yes to the Bridegroom's covenant, you are as she is. You're still in the same tent, this present world. Things around you may look the same and feel the same. Your life, your circumstances may look unchanged. But something very big has changed... you. It is not the tent that has changed, or your world, but you. And so you are no longer of the world. You're in the world, but no longer of it. You no longer belong to your circumstances, nor to your past, nor to your sins and limitations. No longer are you bound to these things. You don't belong to the world. You belong to the Bridegroom. You're free. You're the calah!"*

Henceforth, as worship to God, live every moment of every day as the bride in the tent, belonging to the Bridegroom.

Let the beauty and splendor of your identity as the *Callah*, the Bride of Christ, sink into the recesses of your heart and mind. Let it be a delightful meditation of your heart during your devotional time with your coming Bridegroom.

And carry the profound thought with you that, as human life finds its highest fulfillment in the love of man and woman, so new spiritual abundant life (see John 10:10) finds its highest fulfillment in the love of

God for His sons and daughters and Christ for His church. His bride. His *Callah*. You!

Prepare yourself daily. Moment by moment, make sure you stay ready for Him when He comes back for you.

## CORRECTING OUR IMAGE OF GOD

Cutting right to the chase, know straightaway that we need a paradigm shift of our image of God in the context of proximity – which is defined as:

*Nearness in space, time, or relationship.*

Some synonyms of proximity are closeness, nearness, presence, and adjacency.

I believe I could just stop right here because Holy Spirit Himself is likely illuminating truth to you in real-time as you read this. If so, pause and receive it.

o o o

For the sake of clarity, the word "image" in the context I am using it is defined as *a representation of the external form of a person or thing; to make a representation of the external form of.*

In other words, the picture we have and hold in our minds about God. How we imagine Him. Again, speaking only in the context of proximity, children of God in this present Age of Grace have an incomplete view because of various contributing factors that include:

- Ubiquitous old covenant images and language like *Most High God; The LORD is high above all nations, His glory above the heavens; the LORD who dwells on high; For you are LORD most high above all the earth;* etc.
- Orthodoxy and traditionalism (based on the aforementioned point) that pass from generation to generation
- Artwork and other like cultural depictions

We imagine God as only being "somewhere up there," a far-off distance beyond the sky in the cosmos. Further, even when one may know better than this – which is, the utterly awesome truth that our Omnipresent God lives in us – they still have to constantly work to correct this incomplete view of Him (which shows just how strong imagination and conditioning are).

God charges us to be diligent to present ourselves approved, unashamed workmen who rightly divide His Word of Truth.

Therefore, we must be intentional, accurate, and precise when imagining and cultivating the new covenant image of God in our mind. When we do, this will have a profound effect on our view of Him and thus our views of ourselves in Him – our identity, our strength, our power, our ability, and capability in Him.

As it is written in Luke 17:21, Christ reveals to us:

*God is not far off. He is in you.*
*The Kingdom of God is within you.*

Furthermore, repeatedly throughout Matthew's Gospel, Jesus reveals "the Kingdom of Heaven is at hand."

Yes God sits high above the sky and Heaven is His dwelling place, but He is also in you by virtue of His Omnipresent Spirit.

Correcting our view of Him, corrects our worship of Him. Read that repeatedly and allow it to sink in.

Understanding that God your Creator lives in you – has His abode in your body – causes you to think twice about the things you do in your body. What is and is not acceptable behavior as well as worship of Him.

## VISUALIZATION EXERCISE

Now, with your spiritual mind, absent of any previous ideas, judgment, bias, etc., imagine God being near you instead of far away. Now imagine Him in you. Within your physical being and body.

His name is Yahweh, Jehovah, Elohim, Adonai, Abba, the LORD of Hosts, Holy Spirit, the Spirit of Christ, and Immanuel just to name a few.

The Kingdom of Heaven, spiritual and eternal, is within you. The presence and power of God lives in you. His abode in your body because of these truths:

- Being born again, born of God, born of the Spirit
- Now a spiritual son or daughter of God; like Him
- Now a spiritual heir of God
- Now having full access and authority in the Kingdom of Heaven

As it is written in Matthew chapter 16 verse 19:

> *"And I will give you the keys to the kingdom of heaven, and whatever you bind on earth will be bound in heaven, and whatever you loose on earth will be loosed in heaven."*

Do you see it? Do you really see it? The stunning vision of God being in you and not only in a distant place you go to when your body dies. Ponder how much this changes your perception.

Your perception of your identity and existence in Christ: spiritual sonship and spiritual inheritance; freedom from self and sin; oneness with a reigning King Who has all power and His Spirit lives in you.

Your perception of your power and capabilities that with God all things are possible. Your perception of your past or present circumstances, that you are not what happened or is currently happening to you.

This changes everything. To know and understand God and His Kingdom, the Kingdom of Heaven, is *within* you. Because this is not just a mere vision. No. More than a vision, this is reality. Reality you can access and experience by faith. Lay ahold of it!

## GIVING THESE BODIES BACK UNTO GOD

> *The utmost we can sacrifice and give unto God as an offering to Him is our belief, our obedience, and our bodies as worship.*

To fully believe in Him and His Word. To fully obey Him and His Word. To fully present our bodies as living sacrifices by mortifying our members and living as spiritual and not carnal. Curating what we see and hear through our eye and ear gates, and by doing so, guarding our hearts and minds. Managing how we use our time, talent, and treasure, becoming master stewards over each of these critical areas of responsibility in THESE BODIES.

Also, a big part of it is holiness, with an emphasis on the beauty (keyword) of holiness. Holiness is not what we have been taught in past times, where there are wild restrictions on what is or is not permitted. This is all religious and domination-specific dogmatism that has no association with the truth of holiness in Christ.

Holiness in Christ includes living a life of humility hidden in Him. Dead to self and the world with His Holy Spirit living, moving, being, and acting in you. Working in you incessantly to convict and separate you from sinful behavior, thus invoking full obedience to Him. This is the worship God wants from His people.

## THESE BODIES SET APART "FROM SIN"

When you were (or are now) a new Christian growing in the grace and knowledge of God, learning the Word from hearing teaching and preaching sermons and from reading and studying the bible and other biblical material such as books, devotionals and the like, you've likely learned that to be holy means to be "set apart."

While true, this is an incomplete definition. Most (including myself for many years) do not rightfully learn that to be holy is to be set apart *from sin*. Tragically, the "from sin" part is nowhere to be found in Christian teaching, commentary, and books today. Not surprisingly, given the times we live in where The Great Apostasy, or falling away, spoken of in 2 Thessalonians chapter 2 is unfolding. As it is written:

> *[1] Now, brethren, concerning the coming of our Lord Jesus Christ and our gathering together to Him, we ask you, [2] not to be soon shaken in mind or troubled, either by spirit or by word or by letter, as if from us, as though the day of Christ had come. [3] Let no one deceive you by any means; for that Day will not come unless the falling away comes first, and the man of sin is revealed, the son of perdition, [4] who*

*opposes and exalts himself above all that is called God or that is worshiped, so that he sits as God in the temple of God, showing himself that he is God.*

What is an easily remembered definition of sin? As shared throughout this message, sin equates to THESE BODIES, both being (state) and behavior (actions).

The default, corrupt condition of our bodies of sin which dictates their sinful behavior. Further, sin equates to the spirit of this world and the devil. In sum, the world, the flesh, and the devil as taught to us several places in scripture (Jesus' parable of the Sower, the Temptation of Christ, Ephesians 2:2,3, and James 3:15).

With this, we must turn away from that which is sin by dying to self (shortly, we will get into what this looks like practically) and thereby allowing the Spirit of Christ to live, move and have his way in and through you.

## THE CORE FOUR IN THESE BODIES

I want to emphasize and will keep emphasizing, what I refer to as "The Core Four," which are governing tenets for born-again believers in Christ to live by.

Primarily, God the Father is looking for from us: 1) belief in Him and His Son, Jesus, as Messiah, Savior and LORD; 2) obedience to His Word/Truth; 3) spiritual sacrifices offered to Him; and 4) good works that He predestined us to do before the foundation of the world.

## THESE BODIES

### 1. BELIEF IN HIM

This is ground zero. The starting point for any and everything that relates to salvation and redemption through the finished work of Jesus Christ. You must a) believe God is who He says He is through His Word written (logos) and spoken (rhema); and b) believe Jesus is the Son of God, promised Messiah, and Savior of the world unto eternal life.

As it is written in Hebrews 11:6, *"But without faith, it is impossible to please Him, for he that cometh to God must believe that He is and that He is a rewarder of those who diligently seek Him."*

### 2. OBEDIENCE TO HIM

Obedience to Him is obedience to His Word, which is the same as saying obedience to Truth because God is His Word and He is Truth. There is no separating God from His Word or from the truths of His Word, which is why the bible is referenced as the Word of Truth. Truth is also one of His proper names.

After belief in Him, *full* obedience is an absolute must. Period. Without obedience, your being, body, and behavior are rebellious, making you against God. Making you an enemy of God instead of His child.

As it is written in Matthew 12:30, Christ said, *"He who is not with Me is against me, and he who does not gather with Me scatters abroad."*

True children of God are fully obedient. Keyword, *fully.* So, understand well that obedience and rebellion are the only two locus and they are opposite positions. From God's view, the portrait and characterization of your being and life will be obedience or rebellion. One or the other. This is black and white with zero grey in this matter.

Besides being ubiquitous throughout the entire canon of scripture, the call to obedience is clear and comprehensible for all. No theological exegesis needed. Obedience is as basic as belief in Him and this is His intentional design.

### 3. SPIRITUAL SACRIFICES

Spiritual sacrifices are: belief, faith, trust, hope, obedience, the offering of your body as a living sacrifice, worship, prayer, praise, thanksgiving, and virtuous exchanges such as humility instead of pride, unity instead of division, love of instead of fear, hatred and war, wise instead of foolish, contentment instead of covetousness, self-restraint instead of lust, pure instead of polluted, giver instead of taker, peace instead of worry, calm instead of rage, cheerful instead of depressed, zealous instead of lazy, creative instead of consumer, others-centered instead of self-centered, and so on.

When it comes to sacrifices of praise – a noteworthy spiritual sacrifice in that, over and over throughout the Word of God – we are admonished to give unto God incessantly, without ceasing. I have written an entire book (that will be released after this one) about why this

**THESE BODIES**

is so, but the bottom line is because always praising God removes any and everything evil from the equation.

Further to understand about praise is this: that our old nature will naturally sing the old. Old sad songs of fear, anger, resentment, worry, anxiety, depression, frustration, etc., over what did or did not happen to us (past tense) and/or what is or is not happening to us (present tense).

On the other hand, our new nature in Christ can sing nothing but a victory song. Our new song in Christ is only a victory song. As it is written in 1 Corinthians 15:57, *"but thanks be to God, who gives us the victory through our Lord Jesus Christ."*

The ability to offer sacrifices of praise without ceasing – regardless of your mental, emotional, or physical state; regardless the situation or circumstance – depends upon you being a new (spiritual) creature in Christ. One who has been born of God, born of the Spirit and now uses your body as His abode. This makes spiritual transformation into a spiritual son or daughter, Christ being the firstborn, imperative.

Read this section repeatedly until you really understand it and receive the truth of it in your spirit.

### 4.GOOD WORKS

As it is written in Ephesians 2:10, *"for we are his workmanship, created in Christ Jesus for good works, which God prepared beforehand that we should walk in them."*

God's nature is good, as was all of Creation before the Fall (the event that made man and everything made evil). As a part of God's magnificent plan of redemption that is unfolding from one moment to the next, we, the Body of Christ, are God's workers of good in this world.

If you are truly in Christ, wholly surrendered and fully obedient, there are unique, specific, drawn-out plans of good works for you to carry out for the building of the Kingdom of God, which is an everlasting, spiritual Kingdom made up of spiritual sons and daughters with the risen and ascended Christ as the firstborn.

In closing this *Core Four* section, as I stated in the opening paragraph, these are monumental governing tenets you should be aware of, understand and, in turn, apply. Earnestly study them so you can walk them out.

## LUKEWARMNESS IN THESE BODIES

What I know for sure (because I myself have been guilty several times over throughout my nearly three decades of walking with the LORD), is the fact that our burning love and passion for God and the things of God will wax cold at some point.

God Himself (because there is no separating God from his Word) speaks directly to this evil aspect of our fallen sinful nature through His beloved, chosen and faithful servant John.

**THESE BODIES**

As it is written in Revelation 3:15, the Spirit of the LORD speaks to John in a vision and says: *"I know your works, that you are neither cold nor hot, I will vomit you out of My mouth."*

Lukewarmness. Being neither hot nor cold, as I hang my head down, guilty, and feeling the gentle rebuke and conviction of the Holy Spirit as I write these words. Knowing, by faith, it is because of His love for me and want for my highest good in Him, versus self-centered desires and actions that stem from my sinful nature that, deceitfully, don't feel self-centered and rebellious to the will of God. But isn't that exactly what devilish deception is? Subtle and crafty? You can bank on it.

As much as I would like to, I cannot even say how "cavalier" and "nonchalant" we are about the things of God and truly advancing His Kingdom. I cannot even say how "preoccupied" or "distracted" we are.

Tragically, these adjectives fail to be descript enough. Tragically, what does accurately describe Christians today is the following phrase: *we outright don't fear God enough and therefore don't care enough.* Let me say that again louder for the people in the back:

> *We outright don't fear God enough*
> *and therefore don't care enough.*

Because, tragically, we are too engrossed in our own selves, personal lives, and the lives of others through the lens of social media and other entertainment streaming. Idolatry through and through.

Tragically, we turn lukewarm and stay lukewarm because we take the grace of God for granted, something that is so easy to do because our sinful nature is, by default, rebellious and hostile toward Him in the first place.

Indeed foul. An awful stench in the nostrils of our gracious God and Father. I repent.

## SHIFTING FROM LUKEWARM IDOLATER TO TRUE WORSHIPER

We are not able to offer any worship that is acceptable to God without shifting from lukewarmness and worldliness to worshipper in spirit and in truth.

Separation from self and the world is imperative. Both require dying to self and becoming a living sacrifice that can now, in Christ and with the Spirit of Christ working in you, offer spiritual sacrifices of faith, obedience, prayer/intercession, thanksgiving and praise, and good works.

# 9

# THESE BODIES INVITATION

This invitation is to the Bride of Christ and to the Body of Christ. An invitation for spiritual transformation into a spiritual son or daughter of God, which will, of course, cost you yourself.

This is not the cotton candy, *pretty-with-a-bow-on-top* "gospel" message of what God is about to do for you. No, this is far from the self-centered "gospel" that characterize many Christian messages today.

This is a message from heaven for pure-hearted believers in the holy God of the bible. This is for those who are truly seeking to be and live like Christ. Those who are truly seeking to be the Bride of Christ and thus prepare herself as a bride prepares for her coming bridegroom for final consummation of the marriage.

This is also a message for the Body of Christ to wholly sacrifice self by decreasing so Christ can increase. To fear God and love Him *over and above self* and, as such, to turn away from self and the world and turn to Him.

**APOSTLE TERRI ANDRES**

## WHY WE MUST SACRIFICE THESE BODIES

Why? Have you ever wondered why God the Father wants THESE BODIES unto death – as living sacrifices while we live in them and ultimately through physical death of THESE BODIES? I have showed in great detail throughout this entire message, the answer to this question is rooted in John 4:24 and other related scriptural truths: because God is Spirit, and they that worship Him must worship Him in Spirit and in truth. In other words, *likeness to Him.* God wants His highest creation (man) like Him.

*He wants you and me and all believers in Him like Himself. To be and behave like Him for His glory now and forever.*

The body and spirit are polar opposites, they oppose and war against each other. Spirit versus flesh.

But there is another reason I have not shared until now. I have been waiting for the right time and place to share it and this is it – in this *Invitation* chapter.

That reason is unity. God's ultimate intention for spiritual transformation is perfect and complete unity. Perfect and complete unity between Him and the entire spectrum of His creation – which, of course, includes humanity. Man and the earth. Everything in the earth, under the earth and above it. Atmospheres. The heavens. The moon and stars. Space. Galaxies and everything else within Creation known and unknown.

This perfect and complete unity is not possible for man in the body of flesh. Our superior spirit-man must be set free from its inferior body of sin and corruption.

And for those whose spirits have been made alive through Christ, therefore joined to Him, are then able to be one with the Godhead – God the Father, God the Son and God the Holy Spirit. No longer separated by THESE BODIES of sin and corruption. Rather, joined in perfect and complete unity. Utter oneness. Awesomely one.

This is a painted picture of Christ as the firstborn of many brethren and the Father's mission as it is written in Ephesians chapter 1 versus 10 and 11:

> "That in the dispensation of the fullness of times He might gather together in one all things in Christ, both which are in heaven and which are on earth – in Him."

## A COMPLETE PARADIGM SHIFT IN THESE BODIES

Take a moment and imagine yourself *being* totally different and *living* totally different. Totally different as in the person you see yourself as in the deepest places in your heart and soul. Your highest and best self. Living the life you see yourself living. Your best life in Christ.

It's a good picture, isn't it? That is because God is good and goodness is His will and want for you. He wants you to have new desires. Desires that wholly align with His heart. Not some parts but wholly as in 100%, and only his Holy Spirit living in you, working in you, sanctifying you can cause you to have desires that align with His.

In both the old and new testaments, we see the people of God earnestly desiring Him, earnestly seeking Him, earnestly pursuing Him, earnestly looking to Him, earnestly turning to Him, etc. We see an earnest hunger after Him and, as such, they turned away from the abundant temptations and enticements of the world. They wanted and thus went after different things. Spiritual things and not all the material stuff most Christians today earnestly pursue.

> *God is inviting us to love our life, which is to say love the new life He has given us in Christ to live and walk out for His glory.*

But, by and large, we are so busy loving the lives of others we are constantly looking at and totally missing out on our own life and loving it.

> *When we fully embrace our own and mind our business, we begin to live an extraordinary life.*

The magnificent and joyful life we were meant to live with Him and for Him in terms of serving Him and bringing Him glory.

## THESE BODIES SEPARATION FROM THE WORLD

Something wonderful we can actually do for God is to not be like, look like, and act like the world. Separating ourselves – being, body and behavior – from the world. Like He lovingly commands for our highest good.

*This is part and parcel of holiness.*

Separation from the ideologies, systems and ways of the world and separation from sinful behavior (which the world is chock full of).

God's design is to work through man. Keyword, *through*. Through His holy presence living in you. His abode in your body and, collectively, the Body of Christ. This is one of the reasons the message of THESE BODIES is so imperative for such a time as this.

*God desires and requires holy, honorable vessels.*

Like produces after its kind and therefore responds to its kind. God works through man to win the souls of men. We are co-laborers with God in His field to bring forth His harvest of souls.

God can fully work through us when we are fully available. When we are turned to Him and in order to be fully turned to Him we must be fully turned away from the world. There goes the dichotomy of life again. Another good example of it.

But think about this and marvel over it. That we can be fully used by our Maker. We can be pleasing to Him. God is a miracle-worker. He works miracles all the time. He is always exercising all power and authority. Incessantly, because He never sleeps or slumbers.

By and large, we do not experience the miracles and power of God because we are not holy vessels that He can use. We are astray idolators doing our own thing in the world, like the world.

God is inviting you to something different from this. Something higher. Something greater.

This is no small matter. On the contrary, it is as serious as can be. With where technology is today and where it is going with AI and with the "chokehold" smart phones, social media platforms, and streaming services has on humanity,

The Bride and Body of Christ must be separated and stand out from this. As it is written in Luke 6:43, 44a:

> *For no good tree bears bad fruit, nor again does a*
> *bad tree bear good fruit.*
> *For each tree is known by its own fruit.*

## LUKEWARMNESS IN THESE BODIES

Yes another section on lukewarmness is intentionally included as it needs to be addressed here.

*God is inviting us to be zealous for His house.*

However, unfortunately, we are lukewarm – and by no surprise to God. As it is written in Revelation 3:15, the Spirit of the LORD speaks to John in a vision and says: *"I know your works, that you are neither cold nor hot, I will vomit you out of My mouth."*

He knows our nature and the path we take. He knew in eternity past and now in eternity present that our love for Him would eventually wax cold from our initial burning love for Him when we first, by faith, came to know Him.

One day I asked the LORD why we become lukewarm. He told me because of sin, the sin that lives in us. The longer we live, sin abounds. We sin more and more. So as sin abounds, our love for God waxes cold and we become lukewarm. Lukewarm in that we certainly love God. We acknowledge Him. Worship Him in ways we think are right. And even want to please Him. The issue is we do not love Him *over and above* (key phrase) wanting to do what we please when we please.

What's the remedy? Grace. The grace that is described in Romans 8:2 that says:

*The law of the Spirit of life in Christ has set me free from the law of sin and death.*

This is grace and we know, where sin abounds, grace abounds much more. Therefore, we are no longer under the law, but under grace.

But in order to fully (keyword) benefit from this grace we must wholly surrender our will to His will. Wholly die to self. Wholly believe in Him. Wholly obey Him. Wholly offer spiritual sacrifices to Him. Wholly present our body as living, holy, acceptable sacrifices to Him. So that, through the gift of Grace, He can have His abode in THESE BODIES and thereby perform His good works through us.

## CONSECRATION IN THESE BODIES

You will not be able to shift into the place where God wants you for maximum use unless you consecrate yourself in order to experience His presence and hear from Him.

This consecration is a vital part in receiving this prophetic message in its fullness – understanding it and allowing it to ignite new godly and holy desires, passion, and fire that will ultimately end in your spiritual transformation into a born again (born of God, born of His Spirit) son or daughter of God. A rightful heir through Christ in God our heavenly Father's spiritual household of faith.

*Consecration will open the lines of communication between you and the LORD.*

As you reflect, He will respond. In the end, you will have gained clarity of your current location, or season, which is where you currently are spiritually and, if needed, be in position to confront and conquer deficient areas about your being (character), behavior (actions) and circumstances (consequences of your character and actions). And to be clear, by *deficient* I mean in consideration of Christ – fully surrendered, fully obedient, and fully submitted to His authority – of His Spirit and His Word.

## KEEN FOCUS ON THE WORD IN THESE BODIES

The usage of the word *eyes* in Proverbs 4:21 gives us a clue to what our constant focus should be – on the Word of God. And remember, God is His Word. There is no separating God and His Word, they are One and the same.

Let's take a moment to imagine this. Think about what dominates your focus from day to day. Keyword, *dominates*.

Respectfully, my guess is, it is any and everything but the Word/God. My intention is not to be insulting, so please do not take offense to what will be true for most reading this. Most reading this might think about the Word/God daily in prayer, bible study devotion, etc., but it is not a dominant focus. Keyword, *dominant*.

Here's the thing. Keeping our focus on the Word/God and keeping it in our heart, changes our heart. It transforms our heart and creates in us a new heart. His heart. Why does this matter? Because:

> *Without the heart of God, having His desires, you will never become who you are destined to be in Him.*

Who He designed you to be. Who and what He had in mind when He first thought about you then knit you together in your mother's womb. His spiritual son or daughter, chosen before the foundation of the world, to do good works prepared in advance unto the praise of His glorious grace.

> *You are invited to keep your eyes focused on God and His Word.*

When you do, they will seep into the recesses of your heart and work to transform you from the inside out. Your spiritual inheritance awaits your RSVP to this divine and holy call.

Finally, know that this section was included as one of the last thoughts of this *Invitation* chapter for a reason.

> *The issue of our heart and the desires of our heart is the most important issue as it relates to ourselves and what is within the realm of our control.*

Therefore, it is vital to have the awareness of this and from this awareness to examine your heart and desires. Your desires dictate and thus determine everything. Your passions, beliefs, thoughts, perspectives, attitudes, words, and actions – all of which determine your experiences and outcomes in the moment as well as short- and long-term.

Did you catch all of that? I sure do hope so. Read this section repeatedly to make sure you got it all and that it really, really, really sinks in.

## EDEN EXPERIENCES IN THESE BODIES

Through the finished work of Jesus Christ and redemption we have in Him, I am persuaded that the desire and good pleasure of the Father for His children is to have new moment by moment experiences in THESE BODIES while we yet live in them. What I call Eden Experiences, which are further described as:

> *Extraordinary moments that are good and wholesome and full of unspeakable joy regardless of any external factor outside of yourself.*

I believe this because the decree of God as it is written in Romans 8:37, is that we are more than conquerors through Him that loved us.

When reading the larger context of this verse (verses 18-39), the situation is that of suffering on many levels within and outside of one's self. Yet the individuals experiencing these hardships were *"more than conquerors through Him that loved us."*

> *Eden Experiences require a renewed mind from reading and feeding on the Word of God daily.*

Then further cultivating your new mind through the avenue of your words.

Speaking what you want for yourself – both in quiet calm moments as well as in loud chaotic moments when all hell is breaking loose. Speaking the word of God, which is speaking truth. Speaking what you want to be true. This simple practice is life changing.

> *When you start speaking it, eventually you will experience it.*

Your life and moment by moment experiences will follow your words. Because words really are creative. They carry creative energy because words trace back to God Who is Creator and Author of all things.

## SHOWING UP IN THESE BODIES

In conclusion of this *Invitation* chapter, one thing I know that I know that I know about God is, if we show up in THESE BODIES, He will do the rest.

*Show up in faith as a holy and humble vessel with a pure heart and empty of self.*

Recall to mind two major and amazing metaphors of our faith in God: faith the size of a mustard seed and a little leaven that makes the dough rise.

Mustard trees grow ginormous and continually. Bread starter yeast can literally last forever and make an endless number of loaves. From these we see, with God and our relation to Him, what starts out seemingly insignificant/little/low grows and goes to infinity. Sounds like eternity to me. Hallelujah forever and ever, *El Shaddai!*

How wonderful, magnificent, extravagant, and utterly apropos these two metaphors are in increasing our understanding of this great and mighty God we get to call Father, and I pray you can see, with the eyes of your spirit,

*This beautiful contrast of time and eternity.*
*Of natural order and the superior spiritual order.*

**APOSTLE TERRI ANDRES**

So know and always remember that the particularity of these parables Jesus taught us is very deliberate in meaning (as is all scripture). God wants us to understand that He Himself, His immense, limitless, effectual, and endless mighty power does all the work.

*We need only show up in faith
for Him to show out big through us.*

# 10

# *THESE BODIES FINAL THOUGHTS*

We must take personal responsibility and, moreover, hold ourselves accountable to living virtuously in THESE BODIES. Being Christ-like caretakers of our inner spirit-man by making the right choices in our being/body/behavior, not just sometimes, most of the time. This is everything.

You may think this sounds unreasonable and unattainable. It is not. On the contrary, it is very reasonable and very attainable. We can make good choices and the best choice in the heat of the moment when we hold ourselves accountable and keep ourselves on the hook.

Too, the Word of the LORD also aligns with this thought through the Divine exhortation to *"be ye perfect as I am perfect."* What I know for sure is, if it was impossible to reach perfection in THESE BODIES, with our corrupt condition and all, God would not ask this of us. Doing so would be counter to His character, His Word and instruction in the way of obedience to Him.

Always remember the words of Christ, the Anointed One, as written in Matthew 19:26: *"But Jesus looked at them and said to them, "With men this is impossible, but with God all things are possible."*

The Anointed One has given us His Spirit to enable and empower us to be perfect as He is perfect. We are able to reach this perfection when we live as dead by presenting THESE BODIES as a living sacrifices through our belief in and fear of God, obedience to His Word of Truth and mortifying the misdeeds of our bodies of sin.

## THE CORE FOUR IN THESE BODIES

Over and over throughout the past several chapters, I have been emphasizing "The Core Four," which are governing tenets for born-again believers in Christ to live by.

God is looking for from us: 1) belief in Him and His Son, Jesus Christ as Messiah, Savior, and LORD; 2) obedience to His Word/Truth; 3) spiritual sacrifices offered to Him; and 4) good works that He predestined us (you) to do before the foundation of the world.

### 1. BELIEF IN HIM

This is ground zero. The starting point for any and everything that relates to salvation and redemption through the finished work of Jesus Christ. You must a) believe God is who He says He is through His Word written (logos) and spoken (rhema); and b) believe Jesus is the Son of God, promised Messiah, and Savior of the world unto eternal life.

As it is written in Hebrews 11:6, *"But without faith, it is impossible to please Him, for he that cometh to God must believe that He is and that He is a rewarder of those who diligently seek Him."*

## 2. OBEDIENCE TO HIM

Obedience to Him is obedience to His Word, which is the same as saying obedience to Truth because God is His Word and He is Truth. There is no separating God from His Word or from the truths of His Word, which is why the bible is referenced as the Word of Truth. Truth is also one of His proper names.

After belief in Him, *full* obedience is an absolute must. Period. Without obedience, your being, body, and behavior are rebellious, making you against God. Making you an enemy of God instead of His child.

As it is written in Matthew 12:30, Christ said, *"He who is not with Me is against me, and he who does not gather with Me scatters abroad."*

True children of God are fully obedient. Keyword, *fully*. So, understand well that obedience and rebellion are the only two locus and they are opposite positions. From God's view, the portrait and characterization of your being and life will be obedience or rebellion. One or the other. This is black and white with zero grey in this matter.

Besides being ubiquitous throughout the entire canon of scripture, the call to obedience is clear and comprehensible for all. No theological exegesis needed. Obedience is as basic as belief in Him and this is His intentional design.

### 3. SPIRITUAL SACRIFICES

Spiritual sacrifices are: belief, faith, trust, hope, obedience, the offering of your body as a living sacrifice, worship, prayer, praise, thanksgiving, and virtuous exchanges such as humility instead of pride, unity instead of division, love instead of fear, hatred and war, wise instead of foolish, contentment instead of covetousness, self-restraint instead of lust, pure instead of polluted, giver instead of taker, peace instead of worry, calm instead of rage, cheerful instead of depressed, zealous instead of lazy, creative instead of consumer, others-centered instead of self-centered, and so on.

When it comes to sacrifices of praise – a noteworthy spiritual sacrifice in that, over and over throughout the Word of God – we are admonished to give unto God incessantly, without ceasing. I have written an entire book (that will be released after this one) about why this is so, but the bottom line is because always praising God removes any and everything evil from the equation.

Further to understand about praise is this: that our old nature will naturally sing the old. Old sad songs of fear, anger, resentment, worry, anxiety, depression, frustration, etc., over what did or did not happen to us (past tense) and/or what is or is not happening to us (present tense).

On the other hand, our new nature in Christ can sing nothing but a victory song. Our new song in Christ is only a victory song. As it is written in 1 Corinthians 15:57, *"but thanks be to God, who gives us the victory through our Lord Jesus Christ."*

The ability to offer sacrifices of praise without ceasing – regardless of your mental, emotional, or physical state; regardless the situation or circumstance – depends upon you being a new (spiritual) creature in Christ. One who has been born of God, born of the Spirit and now uses your body as His abode. This makes spiritual transformation into a spiritual son or daughter, Christ being the firstborn, imperative.

Read this section repeatedly until you really understand it and receive the truth of it in your spirit.

### 4. GOOD WORKS

As it is written in Ephesians 2:10, *"for we are his workmanship, created in Christ Jesus for good works, which God prepared beforehand that we should walk in them."*

God's nature is good, as was all of Creation before the Fall (the event that made man and everything made evil). As a part of God's magnificent plan of redemption that is unfolding from one moment to the next, we, the Body of Christ, are God's workers of good in this world.

If you are truly in Christ, wholly surrendered and fully obedient, there are unique, specific, drawn-out plans of good works for you to carry out for the building of the Kingdom of God, which is an everlasting, spiritual Kingdom made up of spiritual sons and daughters with the risen and ascended Christ as the firstborn.

In closing this *Core Four* section, as I stated in the opening paragraph, these are monumental governing tenets you should be aware of, understand and, in turn, apply. Earnestly study them so you can walk them out.

## TRUTH AND HONESTY IN THESE BODIES

One thing that is a must is being honest with yourself. You must take an honest look at yourself and where you are. You must identify your shortcomings and face them. Acknowledge and confront them. Regardless of if this has been an issue for years, recent issue or only sometimes. You cannot conquer what you refuse to confront. Spiritual maturation starts with knowledge/awareness first then truth and honesty.

This process can be quite difficult and uncomfortable, but it is necessary.

For example, in this season of my life, I am experiencing the aftershocks of a major life trauma. As such, I am falling back into old bad patterns. First, recognizing this is key. Second, acknowledging the truth of it is key to interrupting and overcoming these patterns.

## VICTORY SONGS IN THESE BODIES

I cannot emphasize enough the power and value of having and keeping a victory song in our heart versus some outside, external circumstance controlling the song (or the absence of one) in our heart. Having a song in your heart regardless of what is going on within and outside of yourself is evidence of an intimate relationship with your Lord and Savior, Jesus Christ.

A new song is joyful expression for salvation in Christ. A new song is joyful expression for reconciliation back to God and eternal life with Him. A new song is joyful expression for His abode in THESE BODIES. A new song is joyful expression for spiritual transformation, born of God, born of His Spirit. A new song is joyful expression for the Bread of Life, Christ. A new song is joyful expression for the Logos and Rhema Word of God. A new song is joyful expression for wholeness, nothing missing and nothing broken. A new song is joyful expression for power and self-control over every ill of self – fear, frustration, worry, anxiety, anger, addiction, depression, self-centeredness, sluggardness, sexual immorality, shame, pride, covetousness, greed, hatred, offense, unforgiveness, etc. A new song is joyful expression for life in the Spirit. A new song is joyful expression for peace that passes all understanding. A new song is joyful expression for unity and oneness with the Godhead and the brethren in the household of faith. A new song is joyful expression for the future hope and expected end we have in Christ. Glory.

A new song is joyful expression for every promise we have in Christ. As it is written in 2 Corinthians 1:20:

> *The promises of God in Him are yes and amen, to the glory of God through us.*

Amen. Friend, if you didn't know, now you know and now that you do know, make it personal.

What is *your* new victory song? Keyword, *victory*. Go there similar to the way I did above. Really paint the picture. Draw it out. Declare it aloud and commit to donning your victory wreath in Christ by way of incessantly singing your new victory song for the rest of your days. This is my prayer for you, in the name that is above everything named, Jesus Christ. Amen amen.

## DECREEING IN THESE BODIES

Saying what you should be doing. This is so key and is effective in developing self-control and self-discipline.

Research shows, if you say what you should be doing, your actions are likely to follow or start to follow as you say it long enough. Like for me, speaking out loud, I repeat words and phrases like "walk in the Spirit, walk in the Spirit, walk in the Spirit, I am strong, I am strong, I am strong, no, no, no, deny, deny, deny, decrease, decrease, decrease ... " And so many others depending on the moment.

> *The more I speak truth/the Word of God, affirm my new spiritual identity in Christ, and say what I should do, the more I do what I ought to do.*

This encourages self-control and self-discipline in me. I am using my words to change my reality right then and there. This too is effective if we have bad habits and/or addictions that we are trying to overcome.

Streaming too much for example. This is an epic waste of the invaluable gift of time that you and I have been given. Say to yourself, *this is an epic waste of time. I am a creator not a consumer. I want to honor you God, I want to please you God, I want to obey you God by presenting myself to You this moment. Presenting my body as a living sacrifice in this very moment. Offering the faculty of my members unto You right now in this very moment – the eyes of my understanding, ears to hear Your Word and Truth, my mouth to speak your Word to others, the work of my hands to create and write for Thy glory...*

Essentially, recalling to the forefront of your mind, *this is my moment of decision. The oh-so-precious moment of decision that, because of Your grace, is always granted unto me so I get to choose the character of my being and subsequent actions that will follow. Will I feed my old carnal sinful, selfish, rebellious, and disobedient nature? Or* will I deny my old nature and instead feed my new spiritual, holy, righteous, and obedient nature through the Spirit of Christ living in me?

## ROMANS 8:2

> *The law of the Spirit of Life in Christ has set me free from the law of sin and death.*

This has become my life scripture. I remember for years and years being drawn to this scripture. When I came across it in my studies, I would inevitably get sidetracked by it. Giving earnest thought to what it was saying in its surrounding context and in the larger context of what the scriptures teach us. Questioning Holy Spirit and asking Him to reveal His "secret" meaning of it. Secret in that my spirit always knew there was something for me with this scripture. My spirit man knew something my mind could not comprehend.

It was years before He would, but finally in 2017 He did. And instead of only revealing the meaning of it to me, He did far better and gave me the meaning of it by performing the work of it in me. HALLELUJAH!

What I now know from being a living testimony is:

> *This profound scripture reveals the contrast between spirit and flesh/the body of sin. Good and evil. Christ and man.*

**THESE BODIES**

Between the one who:

1. has laid ahold of abundant and eternal life now through belief in God (Yahweh) and a profession of faith in Jesus as His Son and Savior; and
2. while still alive in the body (living dead to self as a living sacrifice), experience freedom from enslavement to the body of sin and its misdeeds that leads to self-destruction and eternal spiritual separation from God the Father upon physical death apart from Jesus Christ.

And the one who has not.

## THE ART OF BEING IN THESE BODIES

Another ultra effective means to overcoming a struggle is to master the art of being, which is how I describe not doing or consuming anything.

When you just be, you are not doing or consuming anything. So, when you've mastered the art of being, you avoid evil and bad matter and behavior.

*To master this, you must learn contentment.*
*Contentment is tied to godliness.*

The bible teaches us in 1 Timothy 6:6 that "godliness with contentment is great gain." A spirit of contentment enables you to just be.

## LESS IS MORE IN THESE BODIES

Less is truly more because when you over-indulge and even just indulge you are conditioning your cravings to want that indulgence. The more you have it, the more you get used to it and it no longer satisfies. You must have more, and more, and more and on and on.

Then, of course, you find yourself in a vicious cycle chasing and consuming this thing that is bad for you. It is so true that pleasure weakens and pain strengthens.

When you practice consuming less, you begin to gain appreciation. First, by becoming grateful for the blessing of having it to consume, and from the space of gratitude you learn less is truly more.

## 3 DIFFERENCE-MAKERS:
## WORDS CONSUMPTION AND CONDITIONING

The difference between success or failure in exercising self-control and self-discipline often boils down to your words in the moment and your overall consumption and conditioning.

What you are saying to yourself, saying the right things that align with your wanted outcomes, as well as asking the right questions such as what do I want *more*? Remind yourself what you want *more*.

Also, consumption and conditioning. Get these in your mind and keep them there. Your success boils down to them. This is vital awareness and it is so important because when you recall what you know (that which is true) in the moment, 9 times out of 10 you will make the right choice. Knowledge is indeed power.

## THESE BODIES AND SELF-CONTROL

Self-control, I believe most of you know, is a fruit of the Spirit. The Holy Spirit. God's Spirit. The Spirit of the LORD.

Frankly, I don't really need to add further thoughts to this section on self-control because the truth that self-control is part of the nature of God has enough weight to put a period on this now.

However, what I will briefly share here (because I've already authored and published a life-changing 300 page book about self-control), is that we need the fruit of self-control to grow in us because our self is naturally uncontrolled. Often, out of control.

Without self-control, our bodies naturally act in ways that are out of control. If we don't control self, we end up controlled by our self, which is wholly corrupt in nature thus actions that will align with this.

The message of THESE BODIES requires self-control. Let me repeat that. The message of THESE BODIES requires self-control. Self-control to not feed the evil ills and demands of your flesh and instead starve it.

Beyond THESE BODIES, self-control is essential for every single aspect of our being and lives. Self-control to not harbor shame, guilt, and/or hard feelings when you offend or are offended. Self-control not to harbor unforgiveness and anger. Self-control not to accept oppressive feelings and emotions akin to your sin nature: depression, worry, anxiety, frustration, and so on.

> *All so you (your self) are free to only fear God, believe in Him, obey Him, and do the good works He prepared in advance for you to do for His glory.*

## THE NECESSARY OCCASION FOR SELF-CONTROL

Be encouraged. Self-control, self-discipline, self-restraint is not natural to us. We must develop it and this development is a frustrating, often long and difficult process of successes and failures.

Even when you become self-controlled, there will still be times when you fall short because of the presence of sin that lives in us and all around us in this dark and fallen world we live in.

While working on this final chapter, the Spirit of the LORD reminded me over again and confirmed it (so really understand and receive this encouragement in your spirit, heart, and mind because it is specifically for you reading these words).

> *Keep yourself encouraged by always remembering, in order to develop self-control, there has to be an occasion for it.*

The important thing is to rise to the occasion when it presents itself. Notice my use of the word "when" and not the word "if." This is because falling short is guaranteed. Not *if* you fall short, but *when* you fall short.

And when you do fall short, don't be discouraged and beat yourself up. This is a satanic trap.

The next occasion for you to rise will present itself.

So, prepare for it by strengthening yourself with spiritual worship and the spiritual practices and strategies I have shared here.

## THESE BODIES AND SELF-DISCIPLINE

Often self-control and self-discipline are thought to be the same but they are not. Self-control is about your being and character and the moment-by-moment choices/decisions/actions you take as a result, whereas self-discipline stems from self-control and is about your consistent choices/decisions/actions that become your routine, regimen and or habits.

You need to know the distinction because you need both. Self-discipline stems from self-control and self-control is about your character. So, to develop and/or increase either one of them, you now know the absolute and inarguable starting point is your character.

Please understand, these nobilities (and all nobility for that matter) start with character. Without addressing and increasing the virtue of self-control in your character, you may be able to exercise self-control and self-discipline to a degree, but it will be a struggle to say the least. A vicious and frustrating cycle of high highs and low lows. Never sustaining success which chips away at your confidence and thereby cause you to sink further into self-defeat and acting badly out of it.

I think of self-discipline as personal law. Just as humanity needs rules and courts of law, we as individuals need it to rule over our unruly and wild propensities.

## WHAT I KNOW FOR SURE ABOUT THESE BODIES

Shout out to the one and only Ms. Oprah Winfrey for popularizing this saying of *what I know for sure* by writing a column in her O Magazine publication under this heading about the lessons she learns from the extraordinary life she lives.

While in a vastly different way, what I know for sure from this extraordinary Romans 8:2 life in the Spirit I live is this:

> *Everything you need and even want is available to you when you turn to God and turn away from the world.*

God's goodness and blessings are right in front of you and all around you. His blessings surround you – not because of you, whether good or bad, but because of who He is – His eternal love, goodness, grace, mercy, truth, and faithfulness.

By and large, the Body of Christ does not experience the blessings of God our Father because we are not in the right alignment – as a spiritual son or daughter of His – to receive them. Instead of being spiritual like Him and turned to Him, we are carnal and turned away from Him; and the reality is this makes us children of the devil. Because in Matthew 12:30, Christ was crystal clear when He said, *"he who is not with me is against Me, and he who does not gather with me scatters abroad."* You are either for Him or against Him – there is no in between.

We may not be murderers but we are idolaters all day. We are worldly, self-centered, self-absorbed, distracted, and bound by our own evil interests, lusts, and worldly desires. Absent of the earnest godly desire we see in the written accounts of the early Church, and if we do have some godly desire, it is not stronger than our worldly, self-serving, and self-pleasing desires.

As any good Father that desires to give everything good to his child, your heavenly Father desires the same and more. He wills to have His abode in you so you can experience His awesome presence, power, and miracles great and small day in and day out.

## ANSWERS FOR THESE BODIES

Biblos is the transliteration for the original Greek word βίβλος. Our LORD Jesus Himself, along with several new testament writers, including John, Matthew,

Mark, Luke, and Paul used this word to reference what was written previously in the scroll of "the book" – a reference to the writings of the Old Testament.

The bible is the answer book to everything true about this life as we know it. *True* being the keyword because most, if not everything, we learn from the world outside the bible is deception.

Therefore, we need to understand the bible is a spiritual book. It is a living, breathing organism that is active in and of itself and active to the reader of it.

*The bible speaks to and activates your inner, spirit man and when you read it from this locus, it becomes something entirely different.*

The whole context of everything changes and you are then able to comprehend its true meaning (applicable to His plan for humanity and the world at large and applicable to you, your being and life) versus a perverted self-centered misinterpretation that is, sadly, normal.

## THANKSGIVING IN THESE BODIES

Second to Christ being our hope of glory as the apropos final thought to share, is thanksgiving.

For over a year now, the Holy Spirit has been and continues to teach me and lead me in the way of thanksgiving. To reveal to me how the subject of thanksgiving warrants position as a foundational pillar

**THESE BODIES**

in our profession of faith as Christian. Religiously and spiritually, thanksgiving should be a top priority.

But, the problem is, too often our emotions and feelings are attached to our worship. Too often they determine it. Too often they dictate it. And now is the time for the Body of Christ to course correct and detach emotions and feelings from our worship and honor of God.

*Because when we shed off all the complex layers life puts on us, when there is just you and no one and nothing else, standing tall in total freedom –*
*no feelings, no frustrations, no family, no relationships, no work, no money, no material possessions, no attachments of any kind –*
*all there is to do at this point is bow down and worship your Creator and coming Savior from the darkness of this age to the light of eternity. All there is to do is worship, praise, and give thanks.*

What a painted picture. And isn't this what salvation is? How Christ came to redeem us, restore us, heal us, deliver us from sin, self, and evil wiles and make us whole children of God, nothing missing and nothing broken. Christ the firstborn of many brethren (you and me).

More than merely "Christian," we are disciples of Christ. Disciplined ones. Discipline and emotion are opposites, and as I write this I recall how I have often said in response to the popular statement "fear is the opposite of faith," that *feelings* are the opposite of faith.

With this truth as the backdrop, we can clearly see and understand thanksgiving is a decision. To give thanks to God is a *decision*, an act of our free will and volition. To willfully, always giving thanks to God. In good times and bad. In neutral times when you are not feeling anything or are nonchalant about everything. Whatever your current physical condition or state. Whatever your emotions or feelings. Whatever the situation and/or circumstances. Always giving thanks to God. At all times. On every occasion. In every way.

> *Thanksgiving is the joyful new song we should be singing incessantly instead of the old sad songs from bondage, brokenness, fear, frustration, hurt, worry, anxiety, depression and so on.*

The finished work of Christ enables rescue and freedom from these soulish ills and if you (being saved from placing your faith in Christ) are not existing and walking in freedom, you need to decrease so He can increase. Decreasing is dying to self, mortifying your members, presenting your body as a living sacrifice, separating from the world and fully obeying the Word — all of which have been covered in great depth.

Going forward, will you be and behave as a mere, emotional "Christian" or will you be and behave as a mature disciple of Christ that makes a decision to give thanks at all times, every day in every way?

## FINISHING IN THESE BODIES

The popular notion of it not mattering how you start, but rather how you finish is true. How you finish is what matters most and if you have ever lost anyone close to you, you will understand this on an equally emotional and profound level when you reflect back on their entire life in view of their last days – how their last days were lived.

I want you to hear me good and get this. That:

> *Your final chapter is what matters. What matters with us as individuals and what matters in the grand scheme of this life as we know it within the cycle of physical life and physical death.*

With every religion there is something beyond this life as we know it. "The big finish," so to speak. For Christians, it is the marriage of the Bride and the Bridegroom, which is a metaphor for the final eternal unification between the Godhead and all who belong to Christ through faith and the deposit of His Spirit.

What will your final chapter be? Know you are writing it daily with your moment-by-moment choices. And as the writer, producer, and actor, you have total control (free will). I pray your final chapter ends well.

**APOSTLE TERRI ANDRES**

# CHRIST THE HOPE OF GLORY FOR THESE BODIES

Indeed, this is what our lives lived by faith in the Son of God, Jesus Christ, comes down to.

This is why we live by faith and not by sight. This is why we strive to live holy and perfect unto God. This is why we strive to fear only Him. This is why we choose to believe and trust Him and His Word instead of the ideas, opinions, and ways of this world. This is why we choose to be and behave like Him. This is why we choose to mortify the misdeeds of our members. This is why we choose to die to ourselves and live sacrificially in service to Him. Because of:

> *The future glory we are promised in Christ. Because of the promised future freedom from every ill within and outside of ourselves. Because of our promised future spiritual bodies absent of sin and corruption. Because of all the future promises in Him that are yes and amen.*

The gates of hell will not prevail against the Church of Jesus Christ. The question is will He know you? Will you be one of His saints that will rise again to judge the world with Him, reign with Him, and live eternally with Him when He comes again?

You have been cordially invited. Yours and mine and the world's invitation for new, abundant life eternal

**THESE BODIES**

and final glorification of THESE BODIES was secured and sent out over 2000 years ago at Calvary. The question is, will you accept this glorious invitation? Will you say yes and thus live in such a way to receive it when the day comes?

If the answer is yes, this final word and exhortation from the Word of God is specifically for you: to wholly rely upon the Person of Holy Spirit living in you and thereby wholly apply His wisdom to every aspect of your being, body, and behavior.

As it is written in 1 Corinthians 2:5-16 [AMPC]:

### Full Reliance Upon
### Holy Spirit and Spiritual Wisdom
### in THESE BODIES

*⁵ So that your faith might not rest in the wisdom of men (human philosophy), but in the power of God.*

*⁶ Yet when we are among the full-grown (spiritually mature Christians who are ripe in understanding), we do impart a [higher] wisdom (the knowledge of the divine plan previously hidden); but it is indeed not a wisdom of this present age or of this world nor of the leaders and rulers of this age, who are being brought to nothing and are doomed to pass away.*

*⁷ But rather what we are setting forth is a wisdom of God once hidden [from the human understanding] and now revealed to us by God—[that wisdom]* which God devised and decreed before the ages for our glorification [to lift us into the glory of His presence].

⁸ None of the rulers of this age or world perceived and recognized and understood this, for if they had, they would never have crucified the Lord of glory.

⁹ But, on the contrary, as the Scripture says, What eye has not seen and ear has not heard and has not entered into the heart of man, [all that] God has prepared (made and keeps ready) for those who love Him [[e]who hold Him in affectionate reverence, promptly obeying Him and gratefully recognizing the benefits He has bestowed].

¹⁰ Yet to us God has unveiled and revealed them by and through His Spirit, for the [Holy] Spirit searches diligently, exploring and examining everything, even sounding the profound and bottomless things of God [the [f]divine counsels and things hidden and beyond man's scrutiny].

¹¹ For what person perceives (knows and understands) what passes through a man's thoughts except the man's own spirit within him? Just so no one discerns (comes to know and comprehend) the thoughts of God except the Spirit of God.

**¹²** Now we have not received the spirit [that belongs to] the world, but the [Holy] Spirit Who is from God, [given to us] that we might realize and comprehend and appreciate the gifts [of divine favor and blessing so freely and lavishly] bestowed on us by God.

**¹³** And we are setting these truths forth in words not taught by human wisdom but taught by the [Holy] Spirit, combining and interpreting spiritual truths with spiritual language [to those who possess the Holy Spirit].

**¹⁴** But the natural, nonspiritual man does not accept or welcome or admit into his heart the gifts and teachings and revelations of the Spirit of God, for they are folly (meaningless nonsense) to him; and he is incapable of knowing them [of progressively recognizing, understanding, and becoming better acquainted with them] because they are spiritually discerned and estimated and appreciated.

**¹⁵** But the spiritual man tries all things [he [a]examines, investigates, inquires into, questions, and discerns all things], yet is himself to be put on trial and judged by no one [he can read the meaning of everything, but no one can properly discern or appraise or get an insight into him].

> ¹⁶ For who has known or understood the mind (the counsels and purposes) of the Lord so as to guide and instruct Him and give Him knowledge? But we have the mind of Christ (the Messiah) and do hold the thoughts (feelings and purposes) of His heart.

Child of God, I pray in the name and authority of Jesus Christ that the eyes of your understanding be enlightened to receive the true meaning of this sacred passage of scripture, so that this truth will transform you into the spiritual son or daughter you were born to become while your spirit-man is housed in its physical body in eager anticipation and earnest preparation for new, abundant life eternal in the everlasting Kingdom of God.

*Apostle Terri Andres*

# THESE BODIES

# AUTHOR NOTE

To all spiritual sons and daughters of *YHWH*:

As an important ending reminder, please know the material presented in this book – the message itself and how it has been presented – is how God gave it to me during the time period I've shared.

If you are reading this note having just finished reading the book, know this prophetic message has been put in book form raw and unfiltered per instruction I received from Holy Spirit to share it *as-is* without me "messing" with it. Hence, the publishing of this material as unabridged.

I fully trust with blind faith, and admonish you in the same way, that Holy Spirit will reveal the extent of this message to you because *it is specifically for you.*

# CLIFF NOTES

Since a lot of significant ground has been covered in this prophetic message to the Bride and Body of Christ for such a time as this – deep revelation; meat not milk – I decided to include brief cliff notes as an aid for comprehension and quick reference. For deep study, you should refer to the chapters of the book and cited scriptures, as well as the index in the back of the book.

## MESSAGE OVERVIEW

- *The Worship God wants is acceptable worship, which is <u>spiritual worship</u>.* (John 4:24; Romans 12:2; Eph 4:23, Romans 8:6)

- *Acceptable <u>spiritual worship</u> is the offering up of THESE BODIES to God in the form of full obedience so that we become like Him and behave like Him.* This is a spiritual offering. How so? Because it renders John 4:24 worship, worship in Spirit and in Truth (in Christ). With this, we arrive at having:

    a. The Person of Holy Spirit's abode in us - the Spirit of Truth and Righteousness. (John 14:17; Rom 14:17; 2 Cor 5:21)

    b. The Spirit of Truth and Righteousness working in us and out of us the Word of God (which is Truth). Every attribute of God and the fruits of His Spirit. The Law of the Spirit of Life in Christ. (John 14; Romans 8:2; Galatians 5:22-23)

    c. The Spirit of Truth enabling and empowering us to rule over THESE BODIES of corruption in order to perform the works of God (good works) predestined to do in Christ before the foundation of the world. (John 14:17; Eph 2:10)

- <u>*Full obedience*</u> *in every area of our 3B Self™ — being, body, behavior.* When we obey Him, we become like Him. To become like Him. To become spiritual. When we are spiritual like Him we can worship Him acceptably. He only accepts spiritual worship. He does not accept legal worship - works of the flesh. Christ has fulfilled the Law and every legal requirement with the death of His Body (which, Christ body is the only Body that could). To obey God is to be spiritual like Him, a true son or daughter born of Him. Spiritually alive, fully obedient and ruling over your corrupted dead body of sin through a) the Law of the Spirit, Holy Spirit living in us empowering us unto good works; while at the same time b) us mortifying our members putting our flesh to death. The Last Adam, CHRIST. To rebel against God (disobey Him) is to be like the first Adam, spiritually dead and therefore separated from God because of the absence of His Spirit. (Matt 3:13-17; Matt 5:17; John 15; John 3; 1 Cor 15:45-49; Romans 8; Col 3:5-11; Eph 2:10)

- *Spiritual Sons and Daughters.* To become spiritual is ultimately to invite the Person of Holy Spirit to have His abode in you AND work in and through you. The Presence of Holy Spirit and Law of the Spirit of Life in Christ. (John 3; John 14; Romans 8:2; 2 Cor 5:17; Ephesians 4; Galatians 5)

- *Sacrificial Giving.* Acceptable worship is always characterized by sacrificial giving. Giving of:

    1. THESE BODIES, our earthen vessels for His abode. To be His temple. Holy sanctuaries. (1 Cor 3:16-17; 1 Cor 6:13-20; Romans 12:1-2)

    2. Our lives, the lives we are living no longer living for ourselves and our self-centered wants and agenda but rather others-centered agenda; putting what God wants for others /His Kingdom

above ourselves. (Acts 2:42-47; Romans 12; 14:7-9; 1 Cor 11:20-26; 2 Cor 5:15)

- ***What acceptable worship is not and what it does not look like.*** Spiritual worship in stark contrast to Legal worship which is what most of us Christians are still offering (largely because of religion, tradition, and lack of knowledge/revelation/rightly dividing Scripture). Legal worship is what we offer to God in our own human effort and good works (e.g., most of the activities of modern-day megachurches and individual ministries).

## MESSAGE KEY POINTS

- **THESE BODIES are <u>for His abode</u>.** An abode is a permanent place where a person lives. A residence. A dwelling place. God wants to and does come to live in THESE BODIES. His Being. His Presence. His Righteousness.

- **THESE BODIES are <u>for His righteous works</u>.**

- **THESE BODIES <u>are the Body of Christ literally and figuratively</u>.** Literally because He in the Person of Holy Spirit literally has His abode (permanent dwelling place) in our bodies. Figuratively because we are many sons and daughters (many body parts)

## THESE BODIES

but one Body united by the Spirit of Christ in each of our bodies, in THESE BODIES.

- ***THESE BODIES qualify us to live in this present age***. Time. Without THESE BODIES we cannot exist in the world. The two most polar extremes of this life are life and death. Bodies are born. Bodies die. THESE BODIES, therefore, are the basis of every aspect of our lives. When we talk about our lives we are really talking about our bodies. Physical existence in this world. In time. Bodies are the basis of our relationship with our self, others, and everything about life. What we do, where we go. Our experience. Our behavior. Our everything. Our mind, our heart, our desires, every single thing.

- ***THESE BODIES* were made for specific purposes**:
    o To be a dwelling place for God's Spirit
    o To be (reflect) the glory of God
    o To worship, praise and thank God
    o To procreate
    o To create, work, and rule over all other creation
    o To receive love and give love
    o To submit to the superior inner man that should be joined to God (for those in Christ)
    o To give of your self, your time, your talents, and your wealth (for those in Christ, His Body, whom He loves)

With this, God wants our body. God wants THESE BODIES. Have you ever wondered why God made man and gave him a body? Why didn't He make man a spirit only? We don't know exactly why. This is one of the great mysteries of God.

But what we do know is, this is His Sovereign design. For man to be spirit, soul and body. Triune like the Godhead.

And because God made us bodies of flesh in His image and likeness, He wants/desires to live in us - which was His original design before the Fall. The Spirit of God was in Adam and Eve before sin separated them. But today, through the Last Adam, Christ, God is now again able to have His abode in our bodies.

He *desires* to live in THESE BODIES so His presence and His Being is with us. Furthermore, He *needs* THESE BODIES to perform His works of Righteousness in the earth. To co-labor with Him to build (set up) His Kingdom here on earth.

Christ came in a body to - catch this - a) speak the words of the Father; and b) do the works of the Father. When the time came to sacrifice His body for us, He told His disciples He (His body) was going away but they would do greater works than He did. What are the greater works? His disciples and all future disciples speaking the words of God and doing the works of God far beyond Israel to the ends of the earth.

Now, the effort is greater because of multiplication. More than one man (Christ) to one nation (Israel). Now, the words (Truth) and works of God (salvation, miracles, signs, and wonders) would be greater because of spiritual sons and daughters of God in Christ taking it to nations. His body had to die so His Spirit could be loosed for us, to descend from on High, to live in us to speak the Word (Truth) and do the works of the Father.

The Kingdom of Heaven, friend, is in you by Spirit of Christ. The Kingdom of Heaven should not be confused with Heaven.

Heaven, the sky above and beyond, is absolutely a real place – the dwelling place of the Godhead, angels, and other spiritual beings.

On the other hand, the Kingdom of Heaven is in you and in me and in all children of God by the Spirit of Christ (Holy Spirit).

The Kingdom of Heaven is in THESE BODIES. By design. By desire. And to a significant degree, by necessity to establish the Kingdom of our God and Father *"on earth as it is in heaven"* in the blessed name above everything named, the name of Jesus Christ, Savior and LORD of all. Hallelujah amen!

# PERSONAL NOTES

**APOSTLE TERRI ANDRES**

**APOSTLE TERRI ANDRES**

**THESE BODIES**

**APOSTLE TERRI ANDRES**

## THESE BODIES

**APOSTLE TERRI ANDRES**

**THESE BODIES**

**APOSTLE TERRI ANDRES**

# THESE BODIES

**APOSTLE TERRI ANDRES**

**THESE BODIES**

**APOSTLE TERRI ANDRES**

**THESE BODIES**

**APOSTLE TERRI ANDRES**

## THESE BODIES

# *INDEX*

## A

Abode, 21, 31, 37, 39, 42, 46, 47, 50, 56, 61, 66, 72, 104, 122, 129, 137, 140, 151, 153, 163, 176, 177, 178, 180
*acceptable* worship, 8, 9, 10, 11, 19, 25, 35, 92, 94, 109, 110, 112, 114, 175, 178

## B

Belief, 28, 36, 101, 102, 103, 111, 114, 124, 126, 127, 128, 148, 149, 150, 157
Body of Christ, 1, 2, 3, 32, 42, 55, 62, 77, 80, 100, 105, 117, 130, 133, 137, 138, 152, 163, 165, 175, 178
Body of sin, 18, 22, 69, 74, 156, 157, 177

Bride of Christ, 46, 117, 119, 133

## C

Carnal
 carnality, 10, 33, 36, 37, 73, 85, 92, 99, 114, 115, 117, 124, 155
Christian, 2, 3, 5, 22, 38, 100, 112, 115, 125, 165, 166
Church, 2, 4, 73, 163, 168
Condition, 17, 18, 79, 80, 81, 82, 83, 84, 85, 86, 89, 91, 92, 100, 106, 126, 147, 166
CONSUMPTION, 85, 97, 158
*Corruption*, 18, 23, 45, 56, 57, 58, 63, 84, 88, 89, 91, 99, 111, 135, 176

## D

Death, 4, 5, 8, 15, 16, 17, 18, 19, 22, 23, 28, 32, 34, 35, 42, 43, 44, 45, 46, 49, 50, 53, 54, 55, 56, 57, 59, 61, 62, 63, 64, 68, 69, 70, 72, 74, 76, 82, 85, 97, 98, 110, 111, 134, 139, 156, 157, 167, 176, 177, 179

Discipline, 70, 105, 106, 154, 155, 158, 160, 161, 162

## E

Evil, 5, 18, 25, 33, 36, 42, 45, 56, 60, 72, 73, 79, 81, 82, 84, 89, 95, 98, 99, 104, 105, 106, 107, 113, 129, 130, 131, 150, 151, 156, 157, 163, 165

## F

*faith*, 8, 22, 28, 42, 55, 56, 61, 62, 63, 64, 70, 72, 102, 103, 124, 127, 128, 131, 139, 140, 144, 145, 149, 150, 154, 157, 165, 166, 173

Father, 3, 13, 23, 27, 35, 37, 38, 39, 43, 48, 62, 63, 68, 73, 101, 105, 110, 126, 132, 134, 135, 140, 143, 145, 157, 163, 180, 181

Flesh, 8, 11, 19, 22, 24, 25, 26, 31, 32, 33, 34, 35, 42, 43, 45, 49, 50, 54, 55, 58, 59, 60, 61, 63, 64, 68, 69, 70, 71, 74, 75, 83, 88, 89, 94, 98, 99, 110, 111, 115, 126, 134, 135, 156, 176, 177, 180

Free

Free will, Freedom, 4, 16, 23, 24, 38, 57, 59, 62, 69, 74, 76, 97, 119, 139, 156, 166

## G

God, 1, 2, 3, 5, 7, 8, 9, 10, 11, 13, 14, 15, 18, 19, 20, 21, 23, 24, 25, 26, 27, 29, 30, 32, 33, 35, 36, 37, 39, 43, 44, 45, 46, 48, 51, 55, 56, 58, 59, 60, 61, 62, 63, 64, 65, 67, 68, 69, 70, 71, 72, 73, 74, 75, 76, 77, 83, 84, 85, 87, 88, 92, 93, 94, 96, 97, 99, 100, 101, 102, 103, 104, 105, 106, 109, 110, 111, 112, 113, 114, 117, 118, 119, 120, 121, 122, 123, 124, 125, 126, 127, 128, 129, 130, 131, 132, 133, 134, 135, 136, 137, 138,

139, 140, 141, 142, 143, 144,
145, 147, 148, 149, 150, 151,
152, 153, 154, 155, 157, 159,
162, 163, 165, 166, 173, 175,
176, 177, 178, 179, 180, 181,
207

Good works, 3, 10, 36, 63, 73,
84, 93, 101, 104, 105, 111,
127, 130, 140, 148, 151, 152,
176, 177, 178

Grace, 95, 111, 121, 139

## H

Heart, 3, 4, 7, 9, 13, 29, 42, 56,
60, 72, 73, 79, 83, 88, 96,
105, 106, 109, 112, 114, 117,
119, 135, 141, 142, 144, 153,
160, 179

Heaven
Kingdom of Heaven, 18, 24,
26, 32, 33, 38, 39, 45, 47,
51, 54, 56, 64, 68, 101,
115, 118, 119, 123, 135

Heir
spiritual heir, 123, 207

Holy, 8, 27, 31, 33, 36, 38, 47,
60, 68, 69, 70, 74, 75, 76, 88,
93, 99, 110, 111, 116, 124,
125, 137, 138, 140, 142, 144,
156

Holy Spirit, 1, 10, 11, 14, 15, 16,
21, 22, 23, 24, 26, 27, 28, 39,
44, 49, 62, 65, 67, 68, 70, 73,
76, 87, 93, 120, 122, 131,
135, 136, 156, 159, 164, 173,
176, 177, 178

## J

Jesus
Jesus Christ, 2, 5, 18, 24, 26,
32, 35, 41, 42, 44, 48, 49,
51, 53, 55, 57, 58, 59, 62,
68, 69, 70, 71, 72, 73, 74,
79, 80, 84, 93, 99, 101,
102, 104, 110, 111, 116,
125, 126, 127, 129, 130,
143, 145, 148, 149, 151,
153, 154, 157, 163

JOINED TO CHRIST, 63

Joy, 83, 143, 153

## K

Kingdom
Kingdom of God, 2, 3, 20,
111, 123

## L

Law, 54, 57, 59, 95, 111, 176, 177
LUKEWARM, 132

## N

New nature, 45, 104, 129, 151

## O

Obedience, 9, 23, 33, 46, 47, 73, 97, 100, 101, 102, 103, 111, 115, 124, 125, 126, 127, 128, 148, 149, 150, 175, 176
Overcome, 37, 95, 98, 155

## P

Peace, 23, 52, 72, 103, 128, 150, 153
Praise, 14, 57, 85, 88, 101, 103, 104, 111, 112, 115, 116, 128, 129, 142, 150, 151, 165, 179
Pray
   Prayer, 43, 55, 65, 112, 145
prophetic, 1, 2, 25, 39, 73, 80, 140, 173, 175
PROPHETIC, 39

## R

Repentance
   repent, 32, 62, 63, 114, 132
Resurrection, 2, 28, 43, 49, 50, 52, 54, 77

## S

Sacrifice, 8, 16, 20, 29, 32, 33, 49, 54, 56, 59, 60, 69, 72, 74, 76, 93, 101, 103, 105, 110, 112, 113, 115, 124, 128, 129, 132, 133, 150, 155, 157, 166, 180
Self, 3, 5, 11, 16, 20, 22, 23, 24, 25, 37, 46, 54, 60, 64, 81, 82, 88, 89, 93, 94, 97, 101, 103, 105, 106, 111, 115, 116, 123, 124, 126, 128, 131, 132, 133, 135, 140, 143, 144, 150, 153, 154, 157, 158, 159, 160, 161, 162, 163, 164, 165, 166, 177, 179, 207
Self-control, 159, 160, 161
Self-Discipline, 161
sinful nature, 16, 56, 61, 83, 131, 132

Soul, 4, 7, 16, 17, 23, 28, 29, 30, 54, 61, 72, 75, 83, 88, 116, 135, 180

*Spiritual sons and daughters*, 3, 2, 3, 24, 37, 38, 63, 65, 73, 92, 93, 99, 105, 116, 130, 152, 173

Struggle, 98, 157, 162

## T

Thanksgiving, 39, 101, 103, 111, 128, 150, 164, 165, 166

THESE BODIES, 2, 1, 2, 13, 14, 19, 20, 21, 22, 24, 25, 27, 28, 30, 33, 34, 35, 37, 39, 41, 42, 43, 45, 46, 47, 50, 53, 54, 55, 57, 59, 61, 63, 64, 65, 66, 67, 68, 73, 74, 75, 79, 80, 84, 85, 86, 87, 88, 91, 92, 93, 94, 97, 99, 100, 105, 106, 109, 111, 124, 126, 133, 134, 135, 137, 140, 143, 147, 153, 159, 161, 176, 177, 178, 179, 180, 181

Transformation

Transform, 3, 25, 72, 83, 84, 92, 93, 94, 95, 100, 104, 129, 133, 134, 140, 151, 153, 207

Truth, 2, 7, 10, 22, 24, 28, 32, 35, 36, 41, 54, 57, 59, 65, 79, 80, 100, 104, 110, 111, 113, 114, 115, 116, 120, 121, 124, 129, 134, 144, 151, 155, 159, 162, 166

## U

Unbelief, 50

Unity, 134

## V

Victory, 18, 19, 25, 104, 129, 151, 153, 154

## W

**Wisdom**

Spiritual wisdom and revelation. Living by faith, 169

Worldly, 5, 97, 99, 114, 163

worship, 7, 9, 10, 14, 19, 20, 47, 72, 100, 103, 109, 110, 111, 112, 114, 117, 119, 122, 128, 132, 134, 150, 161, 165, 175, 176, 177, 178, 179

# APOSTLE TERRI ANDRES